## History Summarized

# KOREAN WAR

WORLD
BOOK

www.worldbook.com

World Book, Inc.
180 North LaSalle Street
Suite 900
Chicago, Illinois 60601
USA

For information about other "History Summarized" titles,
as well as other World Book print and digital publications,
please go to **www.worldbook.com**

For information about other World Book publications, call
1-800-WORLDBK (967-5325).

For information about sales to schools and libraries, call
1-800-975-3250 (United States) or 1-800-837-5365
(Canada).

Library of Congress Cataloging-in-Publication Data for
this volume has been applied for.

History Summarized
ISBN: 978-0-7166-3800-1 (set, hc.)

Korean War
978-0-7166-3804-9 (hc.)

Also available as:
ISBN 978-0-7166-3814-8 (e-book)

Printed in China by Shenzhen Wing King Tong Paper
Products Co., Ltd., Shenzhen, Guangdong
1st printing July 2018

# TABLE OF CONTENTS

Preface: "History Summarized" . . . . . . . . . . . . . . . . . . . . . . . . . . . . . . 4

Introduction: What was the Korean War? . . . . . . . . . . . . . . . . . . . . . 5

Chapter One: History of Korea and causes of the war . . . . . . . . . . . . 6

Chapter Two: The land war . . . . . . . . . . . . . . . . . . . . . . . . . . . . . . . 28

Chapter Three: The war in the air and at sea . . . . . . . . . . . . . . . . . . 58

Chapter Four: Truce and aftermath . . . . . . . . . . . . . . . . . . . . . . . . . 80

Chapter Five: A divided Korea . . . . . . . . . . . . . . . . . . . . . . . . . . . . . 94

Index . . . . . . . . . . . . . . . . . . . . . . . . . . . . . . . . . . . . . . . . . . . . . . . 119

Find out more! . . . . . . . . . . . . . . . . . . . . . . . . . . . . . . . . . . . . . . . 123

Acknowledgments . . . . . . . . . . . . . . . . . . . . . . . . . . . . . . . . . . . . . 124

## "History Summarized"

Each book in this series concisely surveys a major historical event or interrelated series of events or a major cultural, economic, political or social movement. Especially important and interesting aspects of the subject of each book are highlighted in feature sections. Use a "History Summarized" book as an introduction to its subject in preparation for deeper study or as a review of the subject to reinforce what has been studied about the topic.

## What was the Korean War?

The Korean War was the first war in which a world organization, the United Nations (UN), played a military role. The Korean War was a major challenge for the United Nations, which had come into existence only five years earlier.

The Korean War began on June 25, 1950, when troops from Communist-ruled North Korea invaded South Korea. The UN called the invasion a violation of international peace and demanded that the Communists withdraw from South Korea. After the Communists kept fighting, the UN asked its member nations to give military aid to South Korea. Sixteen UN countries sent troops to help the South Koreans, and 41 countries sent military equipment or food and other supplies. The United States provided about 90 percent of the troops, military equipment, and supplies that were sent to South Korea. China fought on the side of North Korea, and the Soviet Union gave military equipment to the North Koreans.

The Korean War ended on July 27, 1953, when the UN and North Korea signed an *armistice* (truce) agreement. A permanent peace treaty between South Korea and North Korea has never been signed. However, United States military forces remain in South Korea to discourage a resumption of hostilities between the two parts of Korea.

The Korean War was one of the bloodiest wars in history. About a million South Korean civilians were killed and several million were made homeless. More than 560,000 UN and South Korean troops and about 1,600,000 Communist troops were killed or wounded or were reported missing.

These ancient paper panels depict the story of the Three Kingdoms of Korea: Goguryeo, Baekje, and Silla.

# CHAPTER ONE

# History of Korea and causes of the war

The Korean War was sparked by the Soviet occupation of North Korea after World War II (1939-1945). However, foreign influence, especially from China, affected much of Korea's early history.

During the last century B.C., several Korean tribes united and formed the state of Goguryeo (or Koguryo) (*goh GOO ree oh*) in the northeastern part of the peninsula. Two other Korean states—Baekje (or Paekche) (*BEHK jay*) in the southwest and Silla in the southeast—were formed at about the same time. Historians call Goguryeo, Baekje, and Silla the *Three Kingdoms.*

In 313, Goguryeo conquered the territory known as Nangnang and took control of the northern half of Korea. Buddhism, which the Koreans had learned about from the Chinese, became the chief religion of the Three Kingdoms in the 300's and 400's. In the 500's and 600's, wars raged among the Three Kingdoms for control of Korea. With the help of the Chinese Tang (*tahng*) dynasty, Silla conquered Baekje and Goguryeo in the 660's and took control of most of the peninsula. (A *dynasty* is a line of rulers belonging to the same family.) Korean art and learning flourished during the next 200 years. The philosophy of Confucianism (*kuhn FYOO shuh nihz uhm*), introduced into the peninsula from China, became a strong influence on Korean thought and behavior.

## Buddhism in Korea

Buddhism (*BU dihz uhm* or *BOO dihz uhm*) is one of the world's major religions. It was founded in India about 500 B.C., or shortly afterward, by a teacher called the Buddha. At various times, Buddhism has been a dominant religious, cultural, and social force in most of Asia. Today, Buddhism has about 350 million followers. Most live in Tibet and other regions of China, and in Japan, the Korean Peninsula, Sri Lanka, and mainland Southeast Asia.

All Buddhists seek comfort, guidance, and security in (1) Buddha; (2) his teachings, called the *dharma*; and (3) the religious community he founded, called the *sangha*. These elements of Buddhism are known as the Three Refuges or Three Jewels.

Buddha is a title given to a person believed to have transcended the cycle of rebirth known as *samsara* and attained *nirvana* (enlightenment). The first Buddha and founder of Buddhism was Siddhartha Gautama, born in the 500's or 400's B.C. in Nepal. Buddhist accounts tell that he was born a prince.

As a young man, after providing for his wife and young son, Gautama resolved to leave his family and palace life to seek spiritual liberation as a wandering *ascetic* (a person who denies himself worldly comforts and pleasures). After traveling throughout northeastern India for six years, Gautama experienced nirvana and discovered the Four Noble Truths. These central teachings state that (1) suffering is part of life; (2) there are causes of suffering, like emotional attachment, ignorance, and selfishness; (3) there is a state of transcendence of suffering; and (4) there is a path that leads to that state. Eventually, Gautama decided to teach his message and founded a community of followers. After others learned of his discovery, they called him the Buddha, which means Enlightened One.

Various Buddhist schools, known as *yana* (vehicles), developed in India and other Asian countries. The Mahayana (*MAH huh YAH nuh*) is the school of Buddhism followed most in the Korean Peninsula. Followers also live in Japan, Tibet, and other regions of China. The word *mahayana* means *great vehicle*. Mahayanists visualize the existence of multiple Buddhas with superhuman qualities. They focus on Buddhas in the heavens and on people

Buddha preached that people can gain nirvana, or salvation, by freeing themselves from worldly attachments and desires. Buddhism began in India and spread to China and other Asian lands.

who will become Buddhas in the future. Mahayanists believe that these present and future Buddhas are able to save people through grace and compassion. The Mahayana ideal of practice is a *bodhisattva (BOH dee SAHT vuh),* a person who vows to become a Buddha by leading a life of virtue and wisdom. At the highest level, a bodhisattva postpones entering into nirvana to work to relieve suffering through acts of compassion.

## Goryeo

In the 800's, Silla broke apart as the kingdom lost control over former Goguryeo and Baekje territories to rebel leaders. But by 935, a general named Wang Geon (*wahng GUN*) (also called Wang Kon) had conquered Silla and the surrounding states and renamed the area Goryeo (or Koryo). The name *Korea* comes from *Goryeo*. The government of Goryeo built schools and encouraged the development of printing to make more books available. The Koreans invented the first movable metal printing type in 1234.

Mongol tribes from the north repeatedly attacked Goryeo from the early 1230's until they conquered it in 1259. Goryeo regained its freedom in 1368 when the Ming dynasty rose to power in China. Two groups, one allied with the Mongols, the other with the Ming dynasty, fought for control of Goryeo. In 1388, a general named Yi Seonggye (*yee SAWNG geh*) led the Ming-

The Three Kingdoms—Goguryeo, Baekje, and Silla—emerged in the last century B.C. A separate region, Gaya, consisted of small town-states. Silla eventually conquered most of the peninsula of Korea.

allied group to victory.

General Yi became king of Goryeo in 1392 and re-named the country Joseon (or Choson) (*JOH son*). Yi founded a dynasty, also called Joseon, which lasted until 1910. Today, Choson is one of the names North Koreans use for their country. South Koreans call their country Daehanmin-guk (*tay HAHN mihn GUK*), often shortened to Hanguk.

Yi and the rulers who followed him reunited

A Joseon dynasty chief (right) sits across from his secretary in this 1818 illustration. The dynasty lasted until 1910.

Korea, reorganized the government, and promoted the arts. In the 1400's, the Koreans regained lost territory and established the northern boundaries of what is now North Korea. But during the 1500's, govern-ment officials and wealthy landowners began fighting for political power. This struggle weakened Korea's government.

Japanese forces invaded Korea in the 1590's, but were driven out with the assistance of Chinese forces. Manchu (*MAN choo*) armies from the north invaded in the 1630's. The Manchus forced Koreans to submit *tributes* (payments), but members of the Yi family continued as kings.

## The Hermit Kingdom

In the 1600's, Korea's rulers closed the country to all foreigners except the Chinese and Japanese. The closure continued for almost 200 years.

## Confucianism

Confucianism (*kuhn FYOO shuh nihz uhm*) is a philosophy based on the ideas of the Chinese philosopher Confucius, who lived from about 551 to 479 B.C. However, some central ideas and values of Confucianism had begun taking shape by the time of the Western Zhou dynasty in China. This *dynasty* (family of leaders) ruled in China from 1045 to 771 B.C. From the time of Confucius to the A.D. 1900's, Confucianism was the most important force in Chinese culture. It influenced art, education, government, literature, personal behavior, and philosophy.

Although Confucianism has religious elements, such as certain rituals, Confucianism has no clergy and does not teach the worship of a God or gods. Confucianism is a philosophy that focuses especially on questions about right and wrong.

In the 500's B.C., when Confucius lived, warfare raged among the many states that made up China. Rapid political change altered the structure of Chinese society, and many people no longer respected the traditional standards of social behavior. Confucius feared that this threat to orderly social relationships would lead to the destruction of civilization.

Confucius believed that society could be saved if it emphasized *moral self-cultivation* in personal and public conduct. Moral self-cultivation is demonstrated by the actions of the *junzi,* meaning *superior person.* Confucius did not define the junzi as an individual of noble birth, but rather as someone with good moral character. Confucius believed that when junzi were rulers, their example would inspire those beneath them to lead good lives.

After Confucius died, his followers spread his ideas. The early

Confucianism has been called both a religion and a philosophy. Its beliefs are widely followed in China and in South Korea. The Confucian believers here worship in a ceremony at the Jongmyo Shrine in Seoul, South Korea.

Confucians concerned themselves primarily with the needs of society. However, ideas from Taoism (*TOW ihz uhm*) and other philosophies helped shift the emphasis to additional areas of human experience.

From about A.D. 200 to 600, interest in Confucianism declined in China. Many Chinese turned instead to Buddhism and Taoism. A revival of interest in Confucianism began in the 600's. The philosopher Zhu Xi (*joo shee*) (1130-1200) became a leader of a movement called Neo-Confucianism. Another influential Neo-Confucian was Wang Yangming (1472-1529).

Although the Chinese Communist government opposed Confucianism in the 1900's, this official opposition ended in 1977. Today, Confucianism remains an important part of Chinese and other East Asian cultures.

Korea was called the *Hermit Kingdom* during this period. Missionaries brought Roman Catholicism to Korea from China in the 1780's. European missionaries first arrived during the 1830's. But Korean authorities persecuted the missionaries and killed thousands of Koreans who had become Catholics.

In 1876, Japan forced Korea to open some ports to trade. Soon thereafter, the United States, Russia, and several European nations signed commercial treaties with Korea. An intense rivalry began for the control of Korea. In 1894, when a rebellion broke out in Korea, China sent troops to end the uprising. Japan also sent troops to protect its growing interests in Korea. The rebellion was crushed, but Japan refused to withdraw its troops. Fighting broke out between China and Japan in July 1894. Japan defeated China in the Sino-Japanese War of 1894-1895, and Japan's influence in Korea became stronger than China's.

The Treaty of Shimonoseki *(SHEE moh noh SEH kee)*, which ended the Sino-Japanese War, granted Korea independence. Japan's victory over Russia in the Russo-Japanese War (1904-1905) forced Russia to recognize Japan's superior influence in Korea. Japan had already owned the Korean railroads and had sent thousands of Japanese settlers to Korea before the war and managed to remove Russian competition in Korea by the war's end. Japan took complete control of Korea in 1910.

## A Japanese colony

The Japanese governed Korea as a colony to benefit their own interests. During the 1930's, the Japanese built many heavy industries in Korea to supply Japan with chemicals, iron and steel, machinery, and other goods. In the 1940's, the Japanese forced the Koreans to take Japanese-style names, and they banned the use of the Korean language in public. Many Koreans were forced to aid the Japanese war effort

The Japanese flag is lowered as Japanese officers and troops formally surrender to the United States at the end of World War II in Seoul, South Korea, in August 1945. The surrender marked the end of the decades-long Japanese occupation of Korea.

during World War II. Some were sent to work in mines and factories inside and outside Korea. Others were drafted into the Japanese military. Some Korean women were forced to work as prostitutes for the Japanese armed forces.

The Allies—the United Kingdom, the United States, the Soviet Union, China, and other countries—defeated Japan in World War II, and U.S. and Soviet forces moved into Korea. After the war, Soviet troops occupied Korea north of the 38th parallel of north latitude, an imaginary line that cuts the country about in half. American troops occupied Korea

## United Nations

The United Nations (UN) is an international organization that works for world peace and security, and for better living standards and human rights for all people of the world. Almost all of the world's independent countries belong to the UN. Each

The United Nations flag has a map of the world surrounded by a wreath of olive branches on a light blue background. The olive branches symbolize peace.

member nation sends representatives to UN Headquarters in New York City, where they discuss and try to solve problems.

The United Nations has two main goals: peace and human dignity. If fighting between two or more countries breaks out anywhere, the UN may be asked to try to stop it. After the fighting stops, the UN may help work out ways to keep it from starting again. But the UN tries above all to deal with problems and disputes before they lead to fighting. It seeks the causes of war and tries to find ways to eliminate them.

The United Nations has met with both success and failure in its work. It has been able to keep some disputes from developing into major wars. The organization has also helped people in numerous parts of the world gain their freedom and better their way of life. The UN works to defend human rights and to provide aid for countries or groups of people in need around the world. For many years, however, disagreements among UN member nations prevented the organization from operating effectively. Since the mid-1980's, greater cooperation among members has enabled the UN to attempt missions in more countries.

The United Nations was established on Oct. 24, 1945, shortly after the end of World War II. As the war drew to an end, the nations that opposed Germany, Italy, and Japan decided that such a war must never happen again. Representatives of these nations met in San Francisco in April and worked out a plan for an organization to help keep world peace. This plan was described in a document called the Charter of the United Nations. In June, 50 nations signed it. They were the first UN members. Since then, over 140 other nations have joined.

In some ways, the UN resembles the League of Nations, which was organized after World War I (1914-1918). Many of the nations that founded the UN had also founded the League. Like the League, the UN was established to help keep peace between nations. The main organs of the UN are much like those of the League. But the UN differs from the League in two main ways. First, all the great military powers except Communist China were UN members from the beginning, and Communist China gained membership in 1971. By contrast, several powerful countries, including the United States, either did not join the League or withdrew from it. Second, the UN's concern with economic and social problems gives it broader responsibilities than the League had.

Six major organs carry on the work of the UN. They are (1) General Assembly, (2) Security Council, (3) Secretariat, (4) Economic and Social Council, (5) International Court of Justice, and (6) Trusteeship Council. Specialized UN agencies deal with such problems as communications, food and agriculture, health, and labor.

The UN has headquarters along the East River in New York City. The flags of all the members fly in front of UN Headquarters.

south of the 38th parallel.

In 1946, when North Korea was still under Soviet occupation, the Communist government took over farmland from wealthy landowners and gave it to farmers who had been living in poverty. The government also took control of most industries.

The United States and the Soviet Union tried to develop a plan for reuniting Korea. They failed, and the United States submitted the problem to the United Nations (UN) in 1947. The United Nations is an international organization that works for world peace and security, and for better living standards and human rights for all people of the world. Almost all of the world's independent countries belong to the UN.

In 1947, the UN General Assembly declared that elections should be held throughout Korea to choose one government for the entire country. The Soviet Union opposed this idea and would not permit elections in North Korea. The Soviet Union refused to allow UN representatives into the North. On May 10, 1948, the people of South Korea elected a national assembly.

## Two Republics of Korea

The assembly set up the government of the Republic of Korea and drew up a constitution. In July 1948, the assembly elected Syngman Rhee (1875-1965) (*SIHNG muhn rhee*) president of the Republic of Korea, which was formed on August 15. On September 9, North Korean Communists established the Democratic People's Republic of Korea. Kim Il-sung (1912-1994) (*kihm ihl sung*) became North Korea's leader.

Both leaders had returned to the Korean peninsula after Japan's defeat in World War II. Kim Il-sung joined the Communist Party while in China in the early 1930's. In the late 1930's and early 1940's, Kim led Korean guerrilla forces against the Japanese in Korea and in Manchuria,

People in Seoul, South Korea, line up to vote in the republic's first free elections in 1948.

a region in northeastern China. Japan had taken control of Manchuria in 1931. In 1940, Kim and his forces retreated to the eastern Soviet Union. Rhee lived in exile in Honolulu, on the U.S. Pacific island state of Hawaii, for 20 years. He returned to Korea after Japan surrendered in 1945. He resigned in 1960 and returned to Hawaii.

Both North and South Korea claimed the entire country, and their troops clashed near the border several times from 1948 to 1950. The United States removed its last troops from Korea in 1949 and indicated early in 1950 that Korea lay outside the main U.S. defense line in Asia. The Communists believed the time was right for military action.

This would test the Truman Doctrine, a policy crafted by the government of United States President Harry S. Truman (1884-1972) to defend countries from Communist aggressors.

## Syngman Rhee

Syngman Rhee *(SIHNG muhn ree)* (1875-1965), a Korean states- man, served as the first presi- dent of the Republic of Korea from 1948 to 1960. He resigned in 1960, soon after his election to a fourth term, because of widespread riots following unfair election practices.

Rhee was born on March 26, 1875, in Hwanghae province, Korea, and was educated in Seoul. Imprisoned from 1897 to 1904 for leading student demon- strations for independence, he wrote the book *Spirit of Indepen- dence* (1904). He then studied in the United States at George Washington, Harvard, and Princeton universities. Rhee lived in exile in Honolulu for 20 years. He returned to Korea after Japan surrendered in World War II (1939-1945), but went back to Hawaii following his resignation. He died on July 19, 1965.

## The United States leads the fight for freedom

Soon after World War II, the Cold War developed between the Soviet Union and its former allies. The Communists gained control over Eastern Europe. Truman realized that the United States would have to lead in the fight for freedom. The country would have to spend as much as necessary to strengthen its war-torn allies. In 1946, Congress approved a $3,750,000,000 loan to the United Kingdom. Then, on March 12, 1947, Truman announced a doctrine of international resistance to Communist aggression. The Truman Doctrine guaranteed American aid to free nations resisting Communist propaganda or sabotage.

The Marshall Plan was outlined by U.S. Secretary of State George C. Marshall (1880-1959) in 1947. It encouraged European nations to work together for economic recovery after World War II. The Marshall Plan extended the Truman Doctrine by proposing that the war-damaged nations of Europe join in a program of mutual aid for economic recovery. They would be assisted by grants from the United States. Communist nations rejected the plan. But 18 other countries accepted it.

In the spring of 1949, the United States, Canada, the United Kingdom, France, and eight other nations signed the North Atlantic Treaty, forming the North Atlantic Treaty Organization. They agreed that an attack on one member would be considered an attack on all. Other countries later joined NATO. The NATO members helped group their armed forces to defend Western Europe. General Dwight D. Eisenhower (1890-1969) served as the first supreme commander of NATO forces.

In 1948, Truman was elected president in an upset victory against Republican Thomas Dewey (1902-1971). In his inaugural address, Truman called for "a bold new program for making the benefits of our scientific advances and industrial progress available for the improvement and growth of underdeveloped areas." In 1950, Congress approved

At a ceremony in the Oval Office of the White House, in Washington, D.C., on Aug. 24, 1949, U.S. President Harry Truman (seated) formally accepted the instruments of ratification and announced that the North Atlantic Treaty was in effect. The United States, Canada, and 10 Western European nations signed the treaty in April 1949. They agreed that an attack on one member would be considered an attack on all.

$35 million for the first part of this Point Four Program. Late in 1951, Truman asked Congress to set up a new foreign aid program for Communist-threatened countries in Southeast Asia. Congress established the Mutual Security Administration to strengthen military defenses in many countries. Western Europe had recovered economically from the war. For that reason, Truman changed the emphasis of foreign aid from economic help to mutual security. He believed that if the nation's allies were strong, America would be strengthened, too.

## Kim Il-sung

Kim Il-sung (*kihm ihl sung*) (1912-1994) headed the government of the Democratic People's Republic of Korea—commonly called North Korea—from 1948, when the country was established, until his death in 1994. He served as premier (later president) and head of the Korean Workers' Party, North Korea's Communist ruling party. Kim led a strict dictatorship, exercising total control over North Korea's armed forces, economy, educational system, and other aspects of society.

Kim was born Kim Sung-ju on April 15, 1912, in Ch'ilgol-dong, near Pyongyang. His father was a schoolteacher. During Kim's boyhood, his family moved to Jilin (also spelled Kirin), China, where he joined the Communist Party in the early 1930's. Around that time, he adopted the name Kim Il-sung. In the late 1930's and early 1940's, Kim led Korean guerrilla forces against the Japanese in Korea and in Manchuria, a region in northeastern China. Japan had ruled Korea since 1910 and had taken control of Manchuria in 1931. In 1940, Kim and his forces retreated to the eastern Soviet Union. In September 1945, after Japan's defeat in World War II (1939-1945), Kim returned to Pyongyang and rose to leadership in the northern branch of Korea's Communist Party.

Kim died on July 8, 1994. The government preserved his body and placed it on display. He was succeeded by his oldest son, Kim Jong-il.

## Truman's critical moments

Harry S. Truman (1884-1972) became president at a critical moment in American history. President Franklin D. Roosevelt (1882-1945) died on April 12, 1945. Truman, a Missouri Democrat, had been Roosevelt's vice president for only 83 days. World War II still had to be won. Plans to establish the United Nations had just started.

When Truman became president, he was known mainly for his work as chairman of a Senate investigating committee. The committee had saved millions of dollars in military contracts during the war. Truman met the challenges of his presidency with courage, determination, and imagination. He made one of the most difficult decisions ever considered by one human being. Truman decided to use the powerful new atomic bomb against Japan to end World War II.

When Truman became president in April 1945, Allied armies were winning the war in Germany. They were preparing to invade Japan. Events moved swiftly. Thirteen days after Truman took office, the first United Nations conference met in San Francisco, California. Then, on May 7, Germany surrendered. Truman proclaimed May 8 as V-E Day (Victory in Europe Day).

In July, Truman traveled to Potsdam, Germany, to confer with Prime Minister Winston Churchill (1874-1965) of the United Kingdom and Premier Joseph Stalin (1879-1953) of the Soviet Union. While in Potsdam, the president received secret word that

American scientists had successfully tested an atomic bomb. On his way home, Truman ordered American fliers to drop an atomic bomb on Japan. The first bomb fell on the city of Hiroshima on August 6. Three days later, a second atomic bomb was dropped on Nagasaki. Truman had believed the United States would have to invade Japan to force that country's leaders to surrender. He and others said dropping the bombs would help end the war more quickly. The bombing thus saved hundreds of thousands of Allied lives while it took the lives of more than 200,000 Japanese people in the two cities. Japan agreed to end the war on August 14. It formally surrendered on September 2.

Truman faced other problems throughout his years in the White House. The United States had to reorganize its economy from a wartime to a peacetime basis. Many war-damaged countries needed relief. Western nations faced Communist aggression in a Cold War that divided the world. To meet these challenges, Truman's administration created some far-reaching programs. They included the Truman Doctrine, the Marshall Plan, the Point Four Program, and the North Atlantic Treaty Organization.

Communist forces from North Korea invaded South Korea in 1950. Truman faced another grave decision. If he sent armed forces to intervene without waiting for United Nations action, he risked war with the Soviet Union. The Soviet Union was a Communist ally of North Korea. But if he delayed, help might be too late. Within two days, the president ordered American armed forces to aid South Korea. His action preserved South Korean independence. It also demonstrated that the United States would support and defend its allies.

U.S. Marines position a machine gun during the Korean War in 1953. The Marine Corps became fully integrated during the Korean War.

## Sphere of influence

Having sowed Communism in North Korea, the Soviet Union created a sphere of influence in east Asia. Just as the Soviets pushed Communism in the eastern bloc of Europe, they quickly rolled it out in North Korea. (A *bloc* is, in this sense, a group of countries combined for a purpose.) The Korean elections stood as an early test of United Nations practices, as well as an example of the Soviets' willingness to keep outsiders from countries where they held sway. Even though the United States had pulled troops out of South Korea, it would return to show leadership in the war as it sought to prevent Communism from spreading to the southern half of the Korean peninsula.

## The war begins

Communist forces from North Korea invaded South Korea on June 25, 1950, starting the Korean War. The United Nations demanded that North Korea withdraw its troops. Truman decided to intervene to save South Korea's independence. On June 27, he announced that he had sent U.S. planes and ships to help South Korea. Congress cheered the announcement. That same day, the UN approved sending troops of other nations to join South Korean and American units. Truman ordered ground forces to South Korea on June 30. The Marine Corps became fully integrated during the Korean War. Truman had signed Executive Order 9981, requiring the desegregation of the military. He later said that sending U.S. troops to South Korea was the hardest decision of his political career. By doing so, he risked starting World War III.

*The U.S. crew of an M24 tank are shown stationed along the Nakdong River front in August 1950. U.S. President Harry S. Truman ordered ground forces to South Korea in July 1950.*

# CHAPTER TWO

# The land war

When North Korea invaded South Korea, the North Korean Army had about 135,000 soldiers. Many of the soldiers had fought for China and the Soviet Union during World War II. North Korea had airplanes, artillery, and tanks. The South Korean Army had about 95,000 soldiers, few planes or heavy guns, and no tanks. At first, the South Korean Army put up little resistance to the enemy attack.

At their greatest strength, the South Korean and UN forces consisted of almost 1,110,000 soldiers. About 590,000 were South Koreans, and about 480,000 were Americans. About 39,000 came from Australia, Belgium, Canada, Colombia, Ethiopia, France, Greece, Luxembourg, the Netherlands, New Zealand, the Philippines, South Africa, Thailand, Turkey, and the United Kingdom.

The North Korean Army grew to more than 260,000 troops during the war. China sent another 780,000 soldiers to help the North Koreans.

On the day the war began, the UN Security Council issued a resolution demanding that the Communists stop fighting and retreat to the 38th parallel. The Soviet Union, which was a member of the 11-nation Council, could have vetoed the resolution. But the Soviet Union was boycotting Council meetings to protest Nationalist China's membership on the Council, and the Soviet delegate was absent when the vote on Korea was taken.

North Korea ignored the UN demand, and, on June 27, its troops reached the outskirts of Seoul, the South Korean capital. That same day, both President Truman and the UN acted to try to halt the Communist advance. Truman ordered U.S. air and naval forces to South Korea and the UN asked its members to aid South Korea. Truman ordered American ground forces into action on June 30. Congress supported Truman's actions and the UN's policy, but did not formally declare war against North Korea.

On July 1, part of the U.S. Army 24th Infantry Division flew from Japan to Busan (*boo sahn*) (also spelled Pusan) at the southern tip of Korea. The next day, these troops began to move into battle positions near Daejeon (*DAY jawn*) (also spelled Taejon), about 75 miles (121 kilometers) south of Seoul. Troops from other UN nations began arriving in Korea shortly after the Americans.

American troops first fought the North Koreans on July 5 at Osan (*OH sahn*), 30 miles (48 kilometers) south of Seoul. The Communists had already captured Seoul.

On July 8, with the approval of the UN Security Council, Truman named Gener-

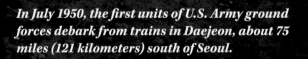

*In July 1950, the first units of U.S. Army ground forces debark from trains in Daejeon, about 75 miles (121 kilometers) south of Seoul.*

## Douglas MacArthur

Douglas MacArthur (1880-1964) was
a leading American general of World
War II and the Korean War. He also
won distinction as Allied supreme
commander of the occupation of
Japan after World War II.

From 1945 to 1951, MacArthur
headed the Allied occupation of
Japan. The occupation had the basic
goals of demilitarizing Japan and
making it a democratic nation. MacArthur administered the
occupation with great independence, and he introduced major
reforms in Japan's political, economic, and social institutions. He
involved the Japanese emperor and government in carrying out
the reforms.

The occupation programs removed from power supporters of
military conquest and reduced the control that a small group of
Japanese families had over the nation's industry. A land reform
program enabled farmers to own their own land. Labor unions
were recognized, the government improved public health and education, and women received the right to vote. A new Japanese
constitution went into effect in 1947. MacArthur also headed the
U.S. Far East Command from 1947 to 1951.

In September 1950, at the beginning of the Korean War,
MacArthur led a surprise landing behind enemy lines at the
South Korean port of Incheon. This move changed the course of
the war, enabling the UN forces to capture Seoul and causing an
almost total collapse of the North Korean army. MacArthur then

invaded North Korea.

Before MacArthur could win a total victory over North Korea, Communist Chinese forces entered the war on the side of the North Koreans. The Chinese drove the UN forces south of the 38th parallel. MacArthur wanted to extend the war into China. But some members of the UN feared that attacking China would start a third world war. MacArthur disagreed with U.S. President Harry S. Truman and the Joint Chiefs of Staff about limiting the war to Korea.

By March 1951, MacArthur's forces held positions close to the 38th parallel. He issued statements criticizing the U.S. government's policy and strategy on the war. MacArthur also sent an unauthorized message demanding the surrender of the Chinese. On April 5, Joseph W. Martin, Jr., a Republican congressman, made public a letter from MacArthur that criticized official policy. (Truman was a Democrat.) On April 11, Truman relieved MacArthur as head of the UN Command, U.S. Far East Command, and the leader of the occupation of Japan. The dismissal created a nationwide furor.

The American public welcomed MacArthur as a hero on his return to the United States. It was his first time back in the country since 1937. However, after a Senate investigation into the reasons for his dismissal, popular support for his position declined sharply.

MacArthur was born in Little Rock, Arkansas, on Jan. 26, 1880. He graduated from the U.S. Military Academy at West Point, New York, in 1903. His memoirs, *Reminiscences,* were published shortly before he died on April 5, 1964.

A group of U.S. soldiers moves up to Busan Perimeter, a battle line in the southeast corner of South Korea, in July 1950.

al Douglas MacArthur (1880-1964) commander in chief of the United Nations Command. The command had authority over all the Allies— South Koreans, Americans, and the troops from other UN countries. MacArthur directed Allied operations from his headquarters in Tokyo, Japan. On July 13, Lieutenant General Walton H. Walker, head of the U.S. Eighth Army, became field commander of the Allied ground forces in Korea.

The U.S. 1st Marine Provisional Brigade and the 2nd Infantry Division of the Army arrived in South Korea in late July. But the Allies were forced back to the Busan Perimeter by August 2. The Busan Perimeter was a battle line in the southeast corner of South Korea. It extended roughly from the city of Pohang on the southeast coast, west around Daegu (*DAY goo*) (also spelled Taegu), and south and southeast nearly to Busan, which served as the temporary capital of South Korea and was the chief landing and supply port of the United Nations forces. The Nakdong (also spelled Naktong) River was the boundary of most of the area.

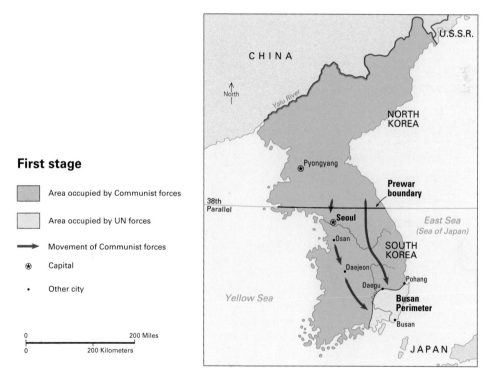

This map illustrates the first stage of the Korean War—the North Korean invasion and advance into South Korea from June to September 1950. Troops from Communist-ruled North Korea first invaded South Korea on June 25, 1950. The United States and several other countries sent troops, equipment, and supplies to South Korea. By August, North Korea had advanced to the Busan Perimeter, a battle line in the southeastern corner of South Korea that extended roughly from the city of Pohang on the southeast coast, west around Daegu, and south and southeast nearly to Busan.

## Marguerite Higgins

Marguerite Higgins (1920-1966) was an American journalist and war correspondent. She shared the 1951 Pulitzer Prize for international reporting for her work in Korea during the Korean War.

Higgins was born in Hong Kong, then a British colony, on Sept. 3, 1920, to an American father and French mother. She and her family moved to the United States when she was a young child. She received her bachelor's degree from the University of California, Berkeley, and her master's degree in journalism from Columbia University in New York City. While at Columbia, she began reporting as a campus correspondent for the *New York Herald Tribune,* and she continued to work for the paper after her graduation in 1942.

Higgins worked hard to persuade the *Herald Tribune* management to send her to Europe to cover World War II. In 1944, the paper sent her to its London bureau. In 1945, she was transferred to Paris and then to locations in Germany. She wrote about the liberation of German concentration camps at Buchenwald and Dachau in that same year. After the war, she stayed in Europe, reporting on such events as the Nuremberg Trials of suspected Nazi war criminals and the Soviet blockade of West Berlin.

In 1950, Higgins became chief of the *Herald Tribune*'s Tokyo bureau, placing her in Asia at the outbreak of the Korean War. Soon after she arrived in Korea, a U.S. military commander banned women from the front. She appealed to General Douglas MacArthur, who headed the United Nations military force sent to defend South Korea, and he overturned the ruling. That Higgins could report from the front was a major victory for women journalists. At that time, women were often assigned to write cooking or society columns, and war reporting was largely seen as a job for men.

After the Korean War, Higgins received permission to travel in the Soviet Union, and there she reopened the *Herald Tribune*'s Moscow bureau. About this time, she joined the paper's bureau in Washington, D.C. In 1963, she accepted a position as a syndicated columnist with *Newsday* and began reporting on the Vietnam War. She contracted the tropical disease leishmaniasis (*leesh muh NY uh sihs*) in 1965, most likely in Vietnam. She returned to the United States for treatment and died in Washington, D.C., on Jan. 3, 1966.

## The Busan Perimeter

The fighting at the Busan Perimeter became a turning point in the war. The North Koreans lost about 58,000 soldiers and much equipment while advancing to the area. The rapid growth of American military strength gave General Walker flexibility in the use of his troops. North Korea tried to break through the perimeter by making scattered attacks along it. Walker reacted by using reserves to meet each enemy thrust, keeping his main defense line intact. Overhead, U.S. planes provided air support and fired at the long enemy supply lines. More American tanks and artillery arrived at Busan to strengthen the defense of the perimeter.

The North Koreans saw that the Allies were gaining military superiority. They mounted a major attack and succeeded in crossing the Nakdong River on August 6. But U.S. Marines and Army forces counterattacked and prevented a general breakthrough. The North Koreans advanced to within shelling distance of Daegu, but major losses of troops and equipment forced them to pull back on August 25. The Communists attacked the Busan Perimeter again on September 3. They captured Pohang three days later, but the Allies halted the enemy advance on September 8.

## The Incheon landing

The Incheon (*ihn chon*) (also called Inchon) landing was a surprise move that changed the course of the war. In mid-September 1950, soldiers of the U.S. X (10th)

In mid-September 1950, soldiers of the U.S. X (10th) Corps, accompanied by U.S. Marines, sailed from Japan to Incheon, on the northwest coast of South Korea. On September 15, the Marines captured the port. The soldiers then came ashore. The Incheon landing was a surprise move that changed the course of the war.

## Sherman tank

The Sherman tank was an armored combat vehicle used by the United States and its allies during World War II and the Korean War. The U.S. Army called it the Medium Tank, M4. It was later named after William Tecumseh Sherman (1820-1891), a Union general in the American Civil War (1861-1865). Sherman tanks were used on nearly all battlefronts of World War II.

Most Shermans carried three heavy machine guns and a 2.95-inch (75-millimeter) gun on a rotating turret. Some Shermans had flamethrowers, hedgerow cutters, larger guns, rocket launchers, smoke mortars, and other modifications. The tanks reached a maximum speed of about 25 miles (40 kilometers) per hour. Sherman tanks carried a crew of five and were used to support *infantry* (soldiers who fight on foot).

Sherman tanks were first tested in 1941. They entered World War II combat with British forces in Egypt in October 1942. They first saw combat with U.S. forces in Tunisia in early December. The tanks accompanied Allied ground forces throughout the rest of the European campaign.

Sherman tanks had success against German tanks in 1942 and 1943. However, later German tanks with thicker armor and larger guns dominated encounters with Shermans. Sherman crews suffered heavy *casualties* (people killed or wounded). But the tanks proved highly effective during the island-hopping campaign against the Japanese in the Pacific.

Nearly every Allied army used Sherman tanks during World War II. Many thousands served with the British and Soviet

Sherman tanks served with U.S. and Allied forces during the Korean War. In this photo, U.S. soldiers prepare to advance along the Han River in South Korea in 1951.

armies. The tanks served again with U.S. and Allied forces during the Korean War. The U.S. Army retired the Sherman tank in the mid-1950's. The tank served in foreign armies until the late 1900's. About 50,000 Sherman tanks were produced, many by Chrysler plants in the Detroit area of the U.S. state of Michigan.

Corps, accompanied by U.S. Marines, sailed from Japan to Incheon, on the northwest coast of South Korea. Incheon had developed into a major port after outside nations forced Korea to open the city and other port cities to international trade in the 1880's. On September 15, the Marines captured the port. The soldiers then came ashore. General MacArthur personally directed the amphibious landing. It required especially careful planning because the tides at Incheon vary more than 30 feet (9 meters). Each boat had to land at high tide because any boat near the shore when the tide dropped would be trapped in mud. The troops who landed at Incheon cut off the North Koreans in the Busan Perimeter area from those north of Incheon.

Commanded by Major General Edward M. Almond, the X Corps moved toward Seoul, 24 miles (39 kilometers) northeast of Incheon. After a bitter battle, MacArthur announced the capture of Seoul on September 26. Meanwhile, General Walker's troops fought their way out of the Busan Perimeter, inflicting heavy losses on the enemy. On September 28, they joined the X Corps near Seoul. MacArthur broadcast a demand for surrender, but North Korea rejected it.

## The Allies move north

Late in September, the Allies prepared to invade North Korea. South Korean troops crossed into North Korea on October 1 and captured the coastal cities of Wonsan, Hungnam, and Hamhung. The Eighth Army troops reached North Korea on October 8 and drove the North Koreans toward Pyongyang (*PYAWNG yang*), the capital. They captured Pyongyang on October 19, and the Communists retreated farther north.

From Pyongyang, the Eighth Army marched through northwestern Korea toward the Yalu (*YAH LOO*) River, the border between North Korea and China. Parts of the X Corps drove through northeastern Korea. Some

Brigadier General Courtney Whitney, General Douglas MacArthur (left to right, front), Brigadier General E. K. Wright (behind MacArthur), and Major General Edward Almond (at right, pointing) observe the shelling of Incheon, South Korea, from the USS *Mount McKinley* on Sept. 15, 1950.

## Lewis Puller

Lewis Puller (1898-1971) was a highly decorated lieutenant general in the United States Marine Corps. He is the only Marine to have received five Navy Cross medals, the second highest decoration for valor in the naval services. Puller's courage was legendary. Nicknamed "Chesty," he became a Marine Corps icon for his leadership both on and off the battlefield.

Lewis Burwell Puller was born in West Point, Virginia, on June 26, 1898. Puller attended the Virginia Military Institute, but he left in 1918 to enlist in the Marine Corps. The United States was involved in World War I (1914-1918) at that time, but the war ended while Puller was still in officer training. In 1919, Puller achieved the rank of second lieutenant, but was then released from active duty. He reenlisted as a private and was sent to Haiti, where the Marine Corps was helping suppress armed rebels opposed to the Haitian government. As an acting officer in command of Haitian troops, Puller gained valuable combat experience. He returned to the United States in 1923 and regained his commission as a second lieutenant the next year.

Puller was sent to Nicaragua in 1928. In 1930, he took command of a company of the Nicaraguan Guardia Nacional (National Guard), a Marine-led force that fought rebels in that country.

Puller and his Nicaraguan troops penetrated deep into rebel territory with no support and won battle after battle against superior numbers. He earned his first two Navy Crosses in Nicaragua, as well as the nickname "Chesty" for his barrel chest and firm determination.

During World War II (1939-1945), Puller fought in several major battles in the south Pacific. He had reached the rank of lieutenant colonel when he led a battalion of Marines in late 1942 during the Guadalcanal Campaign. Puller showed great leadership in the fight and made the welfare of his soldiers a top priority. As a result, his troops liked and trusted him. Puller was promoted to colonel after the campaign at Cape Gloucester on the island of New Britain (now part of Papua New Guinea). He then led the 1st Marine Regiment in the bloody battle to take the island of Peleliu (*PEHL uh lee oo*) in 1944.

During the Korean War, Puller commanded the 1st Marine Regiment through a landing at Incheon (also called Inchon), intense fighting within the city of Seoul, and a bitter winter battle near the Jangjin (also called Chosin or Changjin) Reservoir. His role in these campaigns helped make him a symbol of the strength, courage, and determination of the Marines. Puller retired as a lieutenant general in 1955. He died on Oct. 11, 1971.

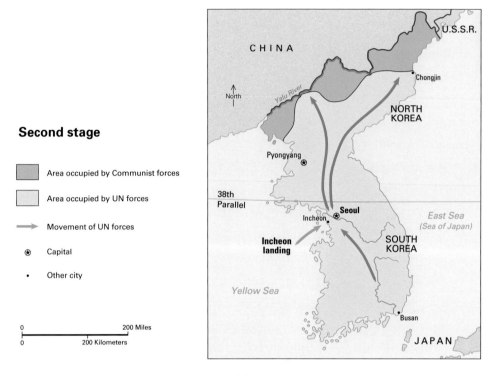

## Second stage

- ▨ Area occupied by Communist forces
- ▨ Area occupied by UN forces
- ➡ Movement of UN forces
- ⊛ Capital
- • Other city

0          200 Miles
0          200 Kilometers

This map illustrates the second stage of the Korean
War—the Incheon landing and the northern advance
of United Nations (UN) troops into North Korea. In
mid-September 1950, when North Korean forces were
in control of much of South Korea, United States
forces made a surprise landing at Incheon, southwest
of Seoul on South Korea's Yellow Sea coast. The U.S.
forces captured Incheon from the North Koreans,
then moved toward Seoul, the South Korean capital,
and captured it as well. In October, UN forces crossed
into North Korea and began to force the North Korean
forces northward. Later that month, the UN forces
captured Pyongyang, the capital of North Korea.
From Pyongyang, the UN forces marched through
northwestern and northeastern Korea. They advanced
as far north as the Yalu River, the border between
North Korea and China.

military experts later criticized this strategy of two commands.

The government of China warned against further advances toward its border. But General MacArthur, hoping to end the war before winter set in, ordered the Allies to press on. U.S. and Chinese troops first clashed on October 25, near the Jangjin (*chawng jihn*) (also called Chosin or Changjin) Reservoir and at Onjong, near Pukchin. They fought until November 6, when the Chinese troops suddenly withdrew. The Allies then pulled back to regroup.

The UN Security Council met to discuss the situation, but the Soviet delegate had returned after previously withdrawing in protest of Nationalist China membership and vetoed any attempt of the Council to act.

MacArthur and his sources of information underestimated the size of the Chinese armies. More than 300,000 Chinese troops crossed into North Korea in October and November. A critical move was an alliance Chinese leader Mao Zedong (*mow zeh dawng*) (1893-1976) had made with the Soviets, who helped strengthen the Chinese army when Chinese forces aided North Korea during the Korean War. MacArthur believed the Allied forces outnumbered the Chinese and that the Chinese would be used for defense only. He also thought that Allied air power could prevent additional Chinese troops from entering North Korea. Political leaders in Washington and most of the Allied commanders shared MacArthur's confidence that the war would be over by Christmas 1950. Allied planes roamed the length of Korea, and Allied warships sailed unchallenged along the coastlines, bombarding enemy ports. MacArthur ordered another advance on November 24.

## The Allies retreat

Hopes for a quick end to the war soon disappeared. China sent a huge

## Matthew Ridgway

Matthew Bunker Ridgway (1895-1993) was one of the greatest combat commanders in the history of the United States Army. He gained fame for leading U.S. forces in some of the most important battles of World War II and the Korean War.

Ridgway was born in Fort Monroe, Virginia, on March 3, 1895. He graduated from the U.S. Military Academy in 1917. He served in China, Nicaragua, the Panama Canal Zone, and the Philippines.

In World War II (1939-1945), Ridgway commanded the Army's famed 82nd Airborne Division during the 1943 invasion of the island of Sicily off the southern coast of Italy and the 1944 invasion of the Normandy region in northwestern France. The Normandy invasion was the largest *amphibious assault*—that is, an attack combining land, sea, and air forces—in history. Ridgway also commanded the XVIII (18th) Airborne Corps during the Battle of the Bulge, in which Allied forces stopped a German advance. The Battle of the Bulge took place in December 1944 in the Ardennes Forest in the countries of Belgium and Luxembourg.

In December 1950, Ridgway took command of the U.S. Eighth Army in Korea. Chinese Communist forces had recently entered the war on the side of North Korea, and the U.S. Army was in retreat. Ridgway reversed the situation and fought back to the 38th Parallel, thus saving South Korea. In 1951, President Harry S.

Lieutenant General Matthew Ridgway, Major General Doyle Hickey, and General Douglas MacArthur (seated left to right as passengers) ride in a jeep at a command post in Yangyang, South Korea, about 15 miles (24 kilometers ) north of the 38th Parallel, on April 3, 1951.

Truman selected Ridgway to replace General Douglas MacArthur as commander of U.S., United Nations, and South Korean forces. In 1952, Ridgway was promoted to full general and supreme commander of Allied forces in Europe.

From 1953 to 1955, Ridgway served as Army chief of staff under President Dwight D. Eisenhower. Ridgway's belief in maintaining a large number of troops to limit the size of potential conflicts put him at odds with Eisenhower, who cut troop numbers and believed in relying more on the threat of using nuclear weapons to prevent a major Communist attack. Ridgway's memoir, *Soldier* (1956), details his position. He died on July 26, 1993.

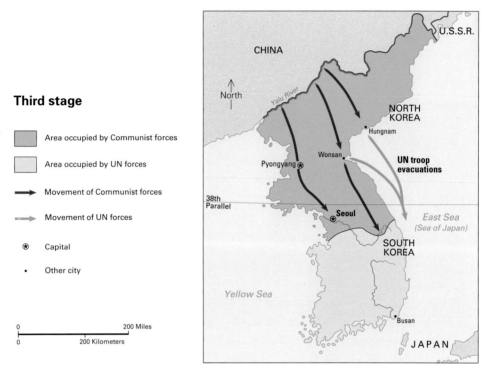

**Third stage**

- Area occupied by Communist forces
- Area occupied by UN forces
- Movement of Communist forces
- Movement of UN forces
- ✵ Capital
- • Other city

0             200 Miles
0          200 Kilometers

This map illustrates the third stage of the Korean War—the Chinese offensive and the retreat by United Nations (UN) forces from November 1950 to January 1951. China, which had entered the war in October 1950, sent a huge force into North Korea and forced the Allies to retreat southward the following month. In December, the Allies began to withdraw from Pyongyang, the North Korean capital. Thousands of UN troops were evacuated by sea from the port of Hungnam on North Korea's east coast. The Communist forces soon crossed into South Korea, and in January 1951, they captured Seoul, the South Korean capital. The Allies' retreat ended about 25 miles (40 kilometers) south of Seoul.

force against the Allies on November 26 and 27 and caused them to retreat. By the end of November, the Communists had driven a wedge between Eighth Army troops in the west and the X Corps in the east. The X Corps had remained independent from the Eighth Army.

The Allies began to withdraw from Pyongyang on December 4. Four

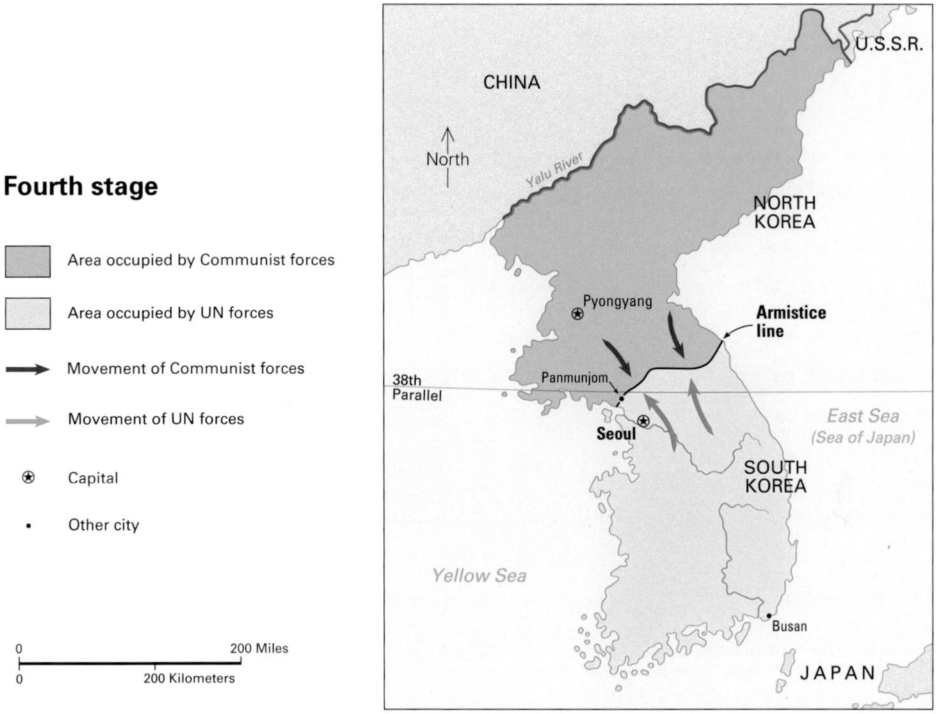
Fourth stage
Area occupied by Communist forces
Area occupied by UN forces
Movement of Communist forces
Movement of UN forces
Capital
Other city
0
200 Miles
0
200 Kilometers
CHINA
U.S.S.R.
North
Yalu River
NORTH KOREA
Pyongyang
Armistice line
38th Parallel
Panmunjom
Seoul
East Sea
(Sea of Japan)
SOUTH KOREA
Yellow Sea
Busan
JAPAN

This map illustrates the fourth and final stage of the Korean War—the advance north by United Nations (UN) troops starting in January 1951, and the battle line north of the 38th parallel where fighting continued between the Allies and the Communists until July 1953. The Allies reoccupied Seoul by March 1951 and some land north of the 38th parallel by June 1951. For the next two years, neither side made important advances but continued fighting for strategic positions. During most of this time, the warring parties held truce talks in Panmunjom, situated in neutral territory between North Korea and South Korea. The map shows the territory each side held when they finally signed an armistice agreement on July 27, 1953.

days later, 20,000 U.S. Marines and infantrymen, surrounded by Chinese, started a historic retreat from the Jangjin Reservoir to the port of Hungnam. By Christmas Eve, 105,000 U.S. and Korean troops, 91,000 refugees, and 17,500 vehicles had been evacuated by sea from Hungnam. In the west, the Communists crossed into South Korea and captured

## Donald Maclean

Donald Maclean (1913-1983) was a British diplomat who worked as a spy for the Soviet Union. He was a member of one of the most damaging spy rings ever uncovered by Western intelligence services, along with Guy Burgess (1911-1963), Anthony Blunt (1907-1983), and Kim Philby (1912-1988).

Donald Duart Maclean was born in London on May 25, 1913, the son of Sir Donald Maclean, a Liberal Party politician and Cabinet minister (that is, a person in charge of a government department, or ministry). He was educated at Gresham's School and Trinity College, Cambridge University. Arriving at Trinity in the 1930's, he met Blunt, Burgess, and Philby. Like them and other young intellectuals of the time, he was attracted to Communism and was recruited to work for Soviet intelligence. Maclean joined the United Kingdom's diplomatic service in 1935. He rapidly advanced to a high position in the foreign office, serving in the British embassies in Paris; Washington, D.C.; and Cairo, Egypt.

Maclean's posting in Washington (1944-1948) proved particularly valuable to the Soviet government. As first secretary and later as head of chancery in the British embassy there, he served as secretary to the Combined Policy Committee on Atomic Development and had access to top-secret information on the United States atom-bomb program. He was also in a position to supply the Soviet government with information concerning the establishment of the North Atlantic Treaty Organization (NATO). After returning from his Cairo posting in 1950, Maclean was appointed head of the American department in the Foreign Office. In this highly sensitive post, he helped in the development of American and British policy for the Korean War.

Donald Maclean (seated on desk, far right) was a British diplomat who helped in the development of American and British policy for the Korean War. He is shown in this 1947 photograph taken at the British embassy in Washington, D.C., with (left to right behind the desk) Second Secretary N. J. Henderson; British Minister to the United States John Balfour; and Head of Chancery W. D. Allen.

By 1951, Maclean was suspected of being a Soviet agent. In May of that year, a joint American and British investigation was about to unmask him when he and Burgess fled from the United Kingdom to Russia, following a warning from Philby. In Moscow, Maclean became a Soviet citizen, working for the Soviet foreign ministry and the Institute of World Economic and International Relations. In 1970, he wrote a book called *British Foreign Policy Since Suez, 1956-68*. He died on March 6, 1983.

Korangpo, 28 miles (45 kilometers) from Seoul.

General Walker was killed in a Jeep accident, and Lieutenant General Matthew B. Ridgway (1895-1993) took command of the Eighth Army on December 27. The Communists began to attack Seoul on New Year's Eve, and they occupied the city on Jan. 4, 1951. The Allies dug in about 25 miles (40 kilometers) south on January 10, and their retreat ended.

## The "Battle for the Hills"

Ridgway quickly restored the confidence of the Allied troops, and they soon inflicted heavy losses on the enemy. The Allies began to move north again on Jan. 16, 1951. In 15 days, they were in position to fire on Seoul. Ridgway used a new tactic calling for slower advances that would wipe out all enemy forces instead of bypassing some.

The Allies reoccupied Seoul on March 14 without a fight. They advanced a short distance into North Korea by June. By then, the war had changed. The two sides dug in and began fighting along a battle line north of the 38th parallel. Truce talks began in July, but fighting continued for two more years. Neither side made important advances, but they fought many bitter battles for strategic positions. During this period, the war was sometimes called the "Battle for the Hills." Battlefields included Bloody Ridge, Finger Ridge, Heartbreak Ridge, Old Baldy, and Pork Chop Hill.

One of the most controversial events of the war took place on April 11, 1951, when President Truman removed General MacArthur from command and replaced him with Ridgway. The president's action resulted from a continuing dispute between MacArthur and defense leaders in Washington as to how the Allies should conduct the war. From the outset, MacArthur had issued public statements that there was no substitute for total victory. He wanted to bomb bases in Manchuria, a part of China, and use other "all-out measures." Truman and his advisers feared such actions

U.S. infantrymen take advantage of cover and concealment in tunnel
positions near the Heartbreak Ridge battlefield in the hills of North Korea,
a few miles or kilometers north of the 38th Parallel, in August 1952.

## William Frishe Dean

William Frishe Dean (1899-1981) was a famous prisoner of war during the Korean War. Dean, a 1922 graduate of the University of California who was born in Carlyle, Illinois, on Aug. 1, 1899, was an American major general who won fame in the early days of the war after North Korean soldiers captured him in 1950 while he was fighting in the front lines. They held him for more than three years as a prisoner of war. He refused to reveal military secrets despite being tortured.

Dean described his war experiences in the popular book *General Dean's Story* (1954). He retired from the Army in 1955 and died on Aug. 25, 1981.

# EXTRA

## San Francisco Chronicle FINAL
### THE CITY'S ONLY HOME-OWNED NEWSPAPER

FOUNDED 1865—VOL. CLXXIII; NO. 85 · CCCCAAA · SAN FRANCISCO, WEDNESDAY, APRIL 11, 1951 · GA 1-1112 DAILY 7 CENTS, SUNDAY 15¢

# MACARTHUR FIRED

## Truman Ousts Him From All Jobs ---Tokyo HQ Stunned by the News

On April 11, 1951, U.S. President Harry S. Truman relieved General Douglas MacArthur as head of the UN Command, U.S. Far East Command, and leader of the occupation of Japan. The dismissal created a nationwide furor. MacArthur was replaced by Matthew Ridgway.

might lead to a third world war. Truman decided he could no longer accept MacArthur's open disagreement with national policy. Ridgway went to Tokyo to replace MacArthur, and Lieutenant General James A. Van Fleet became commander of the Eighth Army.

Partly, Truman saw a need to remove MacArthur due to a disagreement regarding the scope of the war. The Korean War was fought in a limited area on the Korean Peninsula. MacArthur sought to broaden the scope of the war to achieve total victory. Nevertheless, Truman recognized a great risk in MacArthur's desire. Besides, warfare was limited in the air as well as on land. Aerial combat occurred within a confined area because of lines Allied and Communist jet fighters could not cross. Even with those limits, the introduction of jet-to-jet combat opened a new battlefront.

*F-86 Sabre jets are lined up and ready for combat in June 1951. The first battles between jet aircraft occurred during the Korean War.*

# CHAPTER THREE

# The war in the air and at sea

## The air war

The Korean War marked the first battles between jet aircraft. Early in the conflict, Allied bombers and fighter planes based in Japan, Okinawa, and South Korea roared over North Korea unopposed. They supported Allied troops, killed enemy troops, and damaged Communist bases.

The Soviet Union soon began to supply North Korea with MiG-15 jets, and *dogfights*—combat between individual fighter planes at close quarters—became an important part of the war. As many as 100 to 150 U.S. F-86 Sabre jets and Soviet-built MiG-15's took part in some air battles. Each side adopted the principle of *asylum,* which allowed aircraft to withdraw from the battle zone without being pursued.

In November 1950, Air Force F-86 fighters clashed with Soviet-made MiG-15 fighters near the Chinese border along the Yalu River. The U.S. pilots shot down 10 times as many jets as they lost there. When the Korean War ended, the Air Force had downed about 900 enemy planes and lost 139 of its own planes in aerial combat.

All the dogfights occurred over North Korea because Allied planes were not permitted to cross the Yalu River, and the MiG-15's never flew south of the 38th parallel. Most of the battles took place in "MiG Alley," an area between the Yalu and Pyongyang.

Besides the F-86 and MiG-15, fighter jets seen in the Korean War included the P-51 Mustang, which had fought on all fronts in World War

# F-86 Sabre

The F-86 Sabre was a military airplane used by the United States Air Force and its allies during the Korean War. The F-86 was a *fighter jet* (fast-flying airplane with weapons) designed to shoot down enemy planes and attack targets on the ground and at sea. *F* is the U.S. Air Force's designation for a fighter plane. The F-86 was the main U.S. fighter jet of its era. The aircraft famously fought against Soviet MiG-15 jet fighters during the war.

The F-86 Sabre was the first *swept wing* jet fighter used by the U.S. Air Force. Swept wings pointed toward the rear of the aircraft to improve the plane's handling at high speeds. Today, nearly all modern jets use swept wings. The F-86 Sabre was also notable for it large air inlet in the nose and its "all flying" tail that allowed the rear stabilizer to rotate. This helped to make the plane easier to maneuver. The F-86 was developed in the late 1940's. However, it did not enter service until late 1950, shortly after the first MiG-15's appeared in the North Korean air force. (The MiG-15's also used swept-wing technology.) Both fighters outperformed earlier straight-wing jet fighters, and they proved fearsome opponents for each other. Air battles between Sabres and MiG-15's sometimes involved as many as 100 to 150 aircraft. The skies over North Korea where these battles took place became known as "MiG Alley," an area between the Yalu River and Pyongyang, the North Korean capital.

Most F-86 Sabres carried one pilot and six heavy machine guns. The fighter jets were also armed with air-to-air rockets and sometimes bombs and *drop* (fuel) tanks. In later versions, rapid-fire cannons replaced the machine guns. The F-86 had a top

The F-86 Sabre was the fastest U.S. jet used during the Korean War. It was the first *swept wing* jet fighter used by the U.S. Air Force. Swept wings pointed toward the rear of the aircraft to improve the plane's handling at high speeds. Today, nearly all modern jets use swept wings.

speed of nearly 700 miles (1,125 kilometers) per hour. It could reach a maximum altitude of around 49,000 feet (14,935 meters), with a range of about 1,200 miles (1,930 kilometers). In a dive, the F-86 was the first U.S. fighter jet to exceed the speed of sound—761 miles (1,225 kilometers) per hour.

Sabres enjoyed great success in air-to-air combat. They were also used in ground attack and *reconnaissance* (information-gathering) roles. Sabres destroyed more than 800 enemy aircraft—mostly MiG-15's—during the Korean War. Only 78 Sabres were lost in combat. More than 9,000 F-86's, in several different models, were built between 1948 and 1956. The last U.S. Air Force F-86 was retired in 1958. However, the plane served in Air National Guard units until 1970 and in foreign air forces until 1993.

II; the F4U Corsair; and the B-29 Superfortress, which had been used in attacks over the Pacific in World War II.

During the Korean War, U.S. Air Force Captain James Jabara (1923-1966) became the first jet-to-jet combat ace, destroying 15 enemy jets. An *ace* is a pilot who shot down at least five enemy aircraft during a war. Jabara flew an F-86 Sabre jet fighter in the Korean War.

Another star pilot was Daniel James, Jr., (1920-1978), who became the first black four-star general in United States history, achieving that rank in 1975 as a member of the U.S. Air Force. James flew 101 combat missions in the Korean War.

U.S. Marines watch explosions of bombs dropped by F4U Corsair military airplanes during the Battle of Jangjin Reservoir in North Korea, in December 1950.

## P-51 Mustang

The P-51 Mustang was a single-engine fighter plane designed by North American Aviation. It fought on all fronts in World War II. At that time, *P* was the U.S. Army's code for a pursuit plane. Most P-51's carried one pilot and six heavy machine guns, as well as rockets or bombs for surface attacks. A Rolls-Royce Merlin engine gave it a top speed of about 450 miles (724 kilometers) per hour. The P-51 had a maximum altitude around 42,000 feet (12,800 meters). Its range was about 1,000 miles (1,600 kilometers). Drop tanks could double this range. Mustang pilots sat beneath a "teardrop" bubble canopy. This streamlined glass canopy allowed for improved vision.

The P-51 Mustang was a single-engine *fighter* (fast-flying airplane with weapons). It fought on all fronts in World War II before being used in the Korean War.

# Daniel James, Jr.

Daniel James, Jr., (1920-1978) was the first black four-star general in United States history. He achieved that rank in 1975 as a member of the U.S. Air Force.

"Chappie" James was born on Feb. 11, 1920, in Pensacola, Florida. He attended Tuskegee Institute (now Tuskegee University) near Tuskegee, Alabama, and took part in a special training program of the U.S. Army Air Corps (now the U.S. Air Force). Held at Tuskegee Army Air Field, this program trained the men who would become the U.S. military's first black pilots. These men became well known as the Tuskegee Airmen. Many of them fought in World War II (1939-1945).

Daniel James, Jr., flew 101 combat missions as a fighter pilot in the Korean War.

Daniel James, Jr., was the first black four-star general in United States history. He achieved that rank in 1975 as a member of the U.S. Air Force.

In 1943, James received a commission as a second lieutenant. As a fighter pilot, he flew 101 combat missions in the Korean War. In 1957, he graduated from the Air Command and Staff College. He flew 78 combat missions in the Vietnam War (1957-1975), including one in which his team shot down seven enemy MiG fighters, the highest total of the war. James was promoted to brigadier general in 1970 and lieutenant general in 1973. He served as commander of the North American Air Defense Command (NORAD), now the North American Aerospace Defense Command, from 1975 until his retirement in 1978. James died on Feb. 25, 1978.

James spoke out strongly on patriotism and for civil rights. He praised excellence in performance as a way to attack institutionalized racism.

## MiG-15

The MiG-15 was a military airplane used by the Soviet Union and its allies during the Cold War. The MiG-15 was a fighter jet designed to shoot down enemy planes and attack targets on the ground and at sea. MiG-15's most famously flew in the North Korean and Chinese air forces during the Korean War.

The MiG-15 was one of the first swept wing jet fighters used by the Soviet Air Force. The MiG-15 was known for its fast acceleration and high altitude capability. The plane handled well at low speeds and required little space to take off and land. The MiG-15 handled poorly at high speeds, however, and often stalled and spun into fatal dives. Developed in the late 1940's, the MiG-15 entered Soviet service in 1949.

During the Korean War, MiG-15's dominated the early jets and World War II-era aircraft used by the United States and its allies. Soon after the fighter's appearance, however, the U.S. Air Force introduced the F-86 Sabre, which also used swept-wing technology. MiG-15's and F-86's proved fearsome opponents for each other during the Korean War, and air battles between the two sometimes involved more than 100 aircraft. The skies over North Korea where these battles took place became known as "MiG Alley," an area between the Yalu River and Pyongyang, the North Korean capital.

Most MiG-15's carried one pilot and three rapid-fire cannons and optional bombs and drop tanks. The MiG-15 could reach a top speed of 670 miles (1,078 kilometers) per hour and fly as high

During the Korean War, MiG-15 military jets dominated the early jets and World War II-era aircraft used by the United States and its allies.

as around 55,000 feet (16,764 meters). The fighter's range was about 1,100 miles (1,770 kilometers). The Soviet Union built some 12,000 MiG-15's, and thousands more were made in Allied countries. The MiG-15 was used in combat for many years. Some trainer versions of the jet are still in use.

# F4U Corsair

The F4U Corsair was a military airplane used by the United States and its allies during World War II (1939-1945) and the Korean War. The F4U was a single-engine fighter plane designed by the Chance Vought Corporation. *F* was the U.S. Navy's designation for a fighter plane. *U* was a naval code for Vought aircraft. The F4U Corsair was one of the most famous fighters of World War II. *Corsair* is another word for *pirate* or *pirate ship.*

The F4U had a large central propeller and an *inverted gull wing* design. The wings angled down from the body of the aircraft and then curved upward. Seen from the front, the plane's shape resembled a flattened *W.* Short, stout landing gear—suited for rough landings on aircraft carriers—was attached at the bottom points of the *W.* The angled wing design kept the plane's propeller a safe distance above the ground despite the short landing gear.

The Corsair was known for its firepower, ruggedness, and speed. Most F4U's carried one pilot and six heavy machine guns. Some carried four rapid-fire cannons instead of machine guns. Later F4U's had rockets or bombs for ground attacks. An engine made by the Pratt and Whitney Company gave the plane a top speed of over 400 miles (640 kilometers) per hour. The F4U's maximum altitude was over 36,000 feet (11,000 meters). Its range with a drop tank was over 1,500 miles (2,400 kilometers). The plane was designed for carrier service, but many F4U's operated from U.S. Marine Corps island bases.

The Chance Vought Corporation first tested F4U's in 1940. The fighters first entered combat with the Marine Corps in the South Pacific in February 1943. Navy F4U's entered combat in October.

During the Korean War, F4U Corsair military planes flew thousands of combat missions, mainly in ground attack roles.

Corsairs began flying with the United Kingdom's Royal Navy and the Royal New Zealand Air Force in 1944.

During World War II, F4U's flew primarily in the Pacific against Japan. Pilots had great success using them in air-to-air combat, destroying 11 Japanese planes for each Corsair lost. Their ability to carry bombs, rockets, and *napalm* (a jellylike explosive) also made them effective in ground attacks. F4U's provided crucial air support for a number of assaults on Japanese-held islands.

During the Korean War, F4U's flew thousands of combat missions, mainly in ground attack roles. Corsairs also fought for the French in conflicts in Algeria and Indochina (present-day Cambodia, Laos, and Vietnam).

A total of 12,571 F4U's were built between 1942 and 1952. The last U.S. Navy and Marine Corps Corsairs were retired in 1957. Corsairs served in foreign air forces until 1979.

The U.S. Air Force, Navy, and Marine Corps lost more than 2,000 planes during the war. Most of them were shot down by Communist antiaircraft guns. Allied fliers destroyed more than 1,000 Communist planes. Navy and Marine fliers killed about 100,000 Communist troops, and Air Force fliers killed about 184,800.

Late in the war, the Allies equipped bombers with *shoran* (short range navigation), a new navigation technology. The equipment enabled Allied aircraft to make successful bombing raids at night.

The Allies also used helicopters to carry wounded soldiers from battle zones to hospitals. Helicopter pilots made daring rescues of Allied fliers who had been shot down. For the first time, helicopters carried troops into combat.

## Naval warfare

The Allied naval forces included 80 destroyers, 16 aircraft carriers, 8 cruisers, and 4 battleships. The U.S. Navy helped troops land by firing shells at enemy targets on shore. Wonsan, a Communist oil refining and industrial city, was under naval siege for more than two years.

Aircraft carriers and troop transports played roles in holding the Busan perimeter during the first three months of the war. The *Iowa, Missouri,* and *Wisconsin* supported United Nations forces in the surprise attack at Incheon in September 1950. A feature of the ground battles was the success of naval and Marine close air support, with aircraft and infantry operations closely coordinated.

*Iowa*—sometimes called the "Big Stick"—was the first of the last class of U.S. Navy battleships, which also included the *Wisconsin,* the *New Jersey,* and the *Missouri.* These were four of the fastest, most powerful American battleships ever built. *Iowa*, which had patrolled against German warships in the North Atlantic Ocean and later fought the

The USS *Iowa* fires at a North Korean target in 1952. The *Iowa* (sometimes called the "Big Stick") bombarded enemy targets at a number of locations during the Korean War, including Chongjin; Wonsan; Tanchon; Hungnam; and Kojo, near Tongchon. The *Iowa* had patrolled against German warships in the North Atlantic Ocean and later fought the Japanese in the Pacific Ocean during World War II.

The USS *Missouri* (also known as the "Mighty Mo") bombarded enemy targets at Chongjin, Wonsan, Tanchon, Hungnam, and Kojo during the Korean War. It also provided gunfire support at the battles of Okinawa and Iwo Jima and was the site of the Japanese surrender ending World War II.

Japanese in the Pacific Ocean bombarded enemy targets at a number of locations during the Korean War, including Chongjin; Wonsan; Tanchon; Hungnam; and Kojo, near Tongchon.

*Missouri*, which provided gunfire support at the battles of Okinawa and Iwo Jima and was the site of the Japanese surrender during World War II, is sometimes called the "Mighty Mo." *Missouri* also bombarded enemy targets at Chongjin, Wonsan, Tanchon, Hungnam, and Kojo.

*Wisconsin*—sometimes called "Big Wisky"—which had seen action on the Pacific Front of World War II in 1944 and 1945, bombarded enemy targets at Kansong, Kosong, Wonsan, Songjin (now called Kimchaek), and Kojo.

*New Jersey*, which returned to action in 1950 for the Korean War, had been decommissioned in 1948 following many appearances in battle on the Pacific Front during World War II. This was the second *New Jersey* battleship, first commissioned in 1943. The first *New Jersey* battleship was commissioned in 1906 and sank during military bomb tests in 1923. The *New Jersey* is the most decorated battleship in U.S. naval history.

Following the war, these battleships were placed in *mothball* (protective storage) fleets. However, these battleships would be brought out again for later armed conflicts.

Arleigh Burke (1901-1996), who first won recognition during World War II for his excellent handling of destroyers in the South Pacific Ocean in 1943 and 1944, was deputy chief of staff to the commander of naval forces in the Far East during the Korean War.

The Korean War not only brought out new military heroes in aerial and naval action, but also provided training grounds for future military leaders and astronauts. Also, the Korean War saw the return of a few types of fighter jets and battleships that had served in World War II. The parameters of "MiG Alley" and the principle of asylum created structure

## Arleigh Albert Burke

Arleigh Albert Burke (1901-1996) was an American naval officer in World War II (1939-1945). He first won recognition during 1943 and 1944 for his excellent handling of destroyers in the South Pacific Ocean. There he acquired the nickname "31-knot Burke." A *knot* is a unit of speed used for ships and aircraft. His Destroyer Squadron 23, known as the "Little Beavers," covered the

landings on Bougainville, an island in the Pacific Ocean, and fought in 23 separate engagements against the Japanese.

Later, Burke served as chief of staff to the commander, Fast Carrier Task Force 58, Admiral Marc Mitscher. During the Korean War, he was deputy chief of staff to the commander of naval forces in the Far East.

Burke later became a member of the United Nations Truce Delegation. He became a rear admiral in 1950 and served as chief of naval operations from 1955 to 1961. Burke retired from the United States Navy in 1961.

Burke was born on Oct. 19, 1901, in Boulder, Colorado. He died on Jan. 1, 1996, in Bethesda, Maryland. The destroyer USS *Arleigh Burke,* launched in 1989, is named in his honor.

The USS *New Jersey* opens fire on North Korean targets near the
38th Parallel in November 1951. It is the most decorated battleship
in U.S. naval history. It was decomissioned in 1991 and has been a
museum ship since 2001.

for aerial combat. Aerial and naval forces also gave support to ground troops, aiding the success of Allied campaigns. Even with the accomplishments of the air and naval fleets, the end of the war came slowly as the United Nations Command struggled to reach an agreement on issues, particularly those pertaining to prisoners of war.

## From airmen to astronauts

One of the top airmen of the Korean War was John Glenn, Jr., (1921-2016). Glenn, who previously flew 59 missions supporting ground troops in the Pacific Theater of World War II, flew 90 combat missions and shot down three enemy planes. He earned five Distinguished Flying Crosses and 19 Air Medals. Glenn later became an astronaut. He was the first American to orbit Earth, circling the planet three times in

John Glenn, Jr., was one of the top U.S. airmen of the Korean War. As an astronaut, Glenn became the first American to orbit Earth, in 1962.

less than five hours on Feb. 20, 1962. In October 1988, at age 77, Glenn became the oldest person to go into space when he took part in experiments aboard the space shuttle Discovery. He served five terms in the U.S. Senate after being first elected in 1974.

Other future astronauts who flew in the Korean War included the first two moon landers: Neil Armstrong (1930-2012), who completed 78 missions in Navy Panther jets, and Buzz Aldrin (1930-  ), who made 66 missions with the Air Force. Virgil "Gus" Grissom (1926-1967), who flew the first Gemini mission with John Young, flew 100 combat missions during the war, and received the Distinguished Flying Cross and Air Medal. Walter Schirra, Jr., (1923-2007), who participated in the first space *rendezvous* (meeting) in December 1965, flew 90 combat missions for the Navy.

Buzz Aldrin made 66 missions with the U.S. Air Force during the Korean War. Aldrin and Neil Armstrong, who flew 78 missions with the U.S. Air Force during the war, became the first astronauts to land on the moon, in 1969.

Walter Schirra, Jr., flew 90 combat missions for the U.S. Navy during the Korean War. Schirra participated in the first space *rendezvous* (meeting) in December 1965.

*U.S. soldiers stationed in Korea celebrate the Korean War cease-fire, which brought fighting to an end on July 27, 1953.*

# CHAPTER FOUR

# Truce and aftermath

Hopes for peace on the Korean Peninsula increased when Jacob Malik, the Soviet delegate to the UN, proposed a cease-fire on June 23, 1951. On June 30, General Ridgway, acting on instructions from Washington, suggested a meeting between Allied and Communist military officers to discuss a truce.

The truce talks began between the United Nations Command—represented by the United States—on one side, and North Korea and China on the other side on July 10 at Kaesong and were moved to Panmunjom (*pahn moon jom*), which lies in a demilitarized zone, between North Korea and South Korea, on October 25.

A settlement seemed near on November 27, when both sides agreed that the existing battle line would be the final dividing line between North and South Korea if a truce were reached within 30 days. This agreement had the effect of limiting combat, because neither side had much to gain by winning ground it might later have to surrender.

Several issues, especially *voluntary repatriation of prisoners,* prevented a settlement within the 30-day period. The UN Command had insisted that prisoners of both sides be allowed to choose whether they would return to their homelands. Many Chinese prisoners of the Allies had fought against the Communists during the Chinese civil war. They staged a violent protest against a forced return to life under Communism. Some North Korean captives also refused to return home. The Communists could not agree to the UN demand without admitting that

Colonel Chang Chun San (signing, left) of the North Korean Communist Army, and Colonel James Murray, Jr., (signing, right) of the U.S. Marine Corps, initial maps showing the north and south boundaries of the demarcation zone, during cease-fire talks in Panmunjom in October 1951.

Communism had thus far failed to secure the loyalty of all its citizens.

By late April 1952, the truce talks were firmly deadlocked over voluntary repatriation. Fighting continued along the battle line. On October 8, the UN Command adjourned the truce talks, saying the talks would resume when the Communists were ready to offer a helpful suggestion for settling the one remaining issue—voluntary repatriation.

General Mark W. Clark (1896-1984), who led troops in North Africa and Italy during World War II and as general accepted the first German surrender in May 1945, replaced Ridgway as commander in chief of the

## Mark Wayne Clark

Mark Wayne Clark (1896-1984) was a leading United States general of World War II (1939-1945). He also had a major role in the Korean War.

Clark was born in Madison Barracks, New York, on May 1, 1896. He graduated from the U.S. Military Academy in 1917 and served in World War I (1914-1918).

In 1942, during World War II, Clark became a lieutenant general after leading a secret submarine mission to North Africa. He acquired information that was vital to the success of the 1942 Allied invasion of North Africa. Clark commanded the U.S. Fifth Army in its invasion of Italy at Salerno in 1943, during the hard-fought battles at Cassino and Anzio, and during its entrance into Rome in 1944. In 1945, Clark was promoted to general. In May 1945, in northern Italy, he accepted the first major German surrender.

During the Korean War, Clark commanded the United Nations Forces and the U.S. Army in the Far East in 1952 and 1953. He took part in the signing of the armistice that ended the fighting in July 1953. Clark retired from the Army in 1953. He died on April 17, 1984.

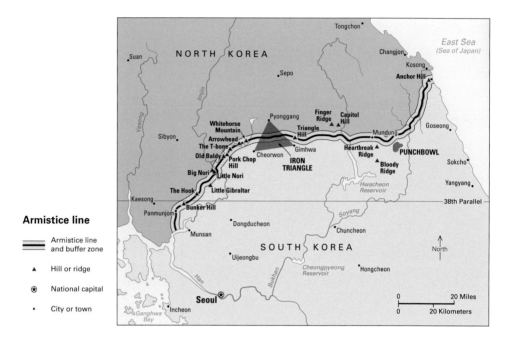

The armistice line between North Korea and South Korea was established by the armistice of July 27, 1953. A demilitarized buffer zone, 2 ½ miles (4 kilometers) wide, was created along the final battle line. Panmunjom, which lies within the buffer zone, was the site of the talks that led to the armistice. The map shows many hills and ridges that were the scenes of bitter fighting.

United Nations Command in May 1952. Dwight D. Eisenhower became president of the United States in January 1953. Then, on March 5, 1953, Soviet premier Joseph Stalin died. After Stalin's death, Soviet leaders began talking of the need to settle disputes peacefully. On March 28, the Communists accepted an earlier offer by the UN Command for an exchange of sick and wounded prisoners. Also, the Communists indicated that the truce talks should be resumed. The exchange took place in April and May. The UN Command received 684 sick and wounded prisoners, including 149 Americans. It returned 6,670 Communist prisoners.

The truce talks began again on April 26, and the Communists accepted voluntary repatriation. They agreed to let prisoners indicate their choice to the Neutral Nations' Repatriation Commission, which consisted of representatives of Czechoslovakia (today the nations of the Czech Republic and Slovakia), India, Poland, Sweden, and Switzerland.

An armistice agreement was signed on July 27, 1953, and the fighting ended. A buffer zone, called the *Demilitarized Zone,* divided the two sides. It was 2.5 miles (4 kilometers) wide along the final battle line. South Korea gained about 1,500 square miles (3,880 square kilometers) of territory. Both sides agreed not to increase their military strength. A Military Armistice Commission, with representatives from both sides, was set up to enforce the armistice terms. The armistice also provided for a political conference to work out a final settlement.

During the war, the United States accused the Chinese and North Korean forces of war crimes against UN troops and South Korean

## Military casualties in the Korean War

| Country | Total casualties | Dead or wounded | Prisoners or missing |
|---|---|---|---|
| UN military casualties | | | |
| **South Korea** | 400,167 | 58,127 dead; 175,743 wounded | 166,297 |
| **United States** | 144,978 | 36,516 dead; 103,284 wounded | 5,178 |
| **Other United Nations** | 17,260 | 3,194 dead; 11,297 wounded | 2,769 |
| **Total** | **562,405** | **97,837 dead; 290,324 wounded** | **174,244** |
| Communist military casualties | | | |
| **China** | 967,000 | 945,000 | 22,000 |
| **North Korea** | 624,000 | 522,000 | 102,000 |
| **Total** | **1,591,000** | **1,467,000** | **124,000** |

## Panmunjom

Panmunjom (*pahn moon jom*) is the site of the truce talks that ended the Korean War in 1953. It lies in a neutral area, called the *Demilitarized Zone,* between North Korea and South Korea. Before the truce talks, Panmunjom was a small civilian village. Today, it is the point of contact between North and South Korea, and between United States and North Korean military representatives. The Panmunjom area is guarded by North Korean forces on the north side, and South Korean and U.S. troops on the south side.

The Korean War truce talks took place between the United Nations Command—represented by the United States—on one side, and North Korea and China on the other side. The talks began in July 1951 in Kaesong, a city under North Korean control. In October, the talks were moved to Panmunjom, in neutral territory. The talks led to the signing of a truce agreement on July 27, 1953.

Panmunjom lies in a neutral area, called the Demilitarized Zone. It is guarded by North Korean forces on the north side, and South Korean and U.S. troops on the south side.

# Highlights of the Korean War

| 1950 | |
|---|---|
| **June 25** | North Korean Communist troops invaded South Korea. The UN demanded that North Korea halt the action. |
| **June 27** | President Truman ordered U.S. air and naval forces to help defend South Korea. The UN asked member nations to aid South Korea. |
| **June 30** | Truman ordered U.S. ground troops to South Korea. |
| **Sept. 8** | Allied troops stopped the deepest Communist advance, at the Busan Perimeter in southeastern South Korea. |
| **Sept. 15** | Allied troops landed behind the enemy lines at Incheon. |
| **Sept. 26** | General MacArthur, commander of UN forces, announced the capture of Seoul, the South Korean capital. |
| **Oct. 19** | The Allies captured Pyongyang, the capital of North Korea. |
| **Oct. 25** | China entered the war on the side of North Korea. |
| **Nov. 26** | The Allies began to retreat after an attack by the Chinese. |
| **1951** | |
| **Jan. 4** | The Communists occupied Seoul. |
| **March 14** | The Allies reoccupied Seoul after ending their retreat. |
| **April 11** | Truman removed MacArthur and replaced him with General Ridgway. |
| **July 10** | Truce talks began, but fighting continued. |
| **1952** | |
| **April 28** | Communist negotiators rejected a proposal for voluntary repatriation of prisoners. |
| **Oct. 8** | The truce talks were broken off. |
| **1953** | |
| **March 28** | The Communists accepted a UN proposal to exchange sick and wounded prisoners. |
| **April 26** | The truce talks were resumed. |
| **July 27** | An armistice agreement was signed, and the fighting ended. |

## The Korean War Veterans Memorial

The Korean War Veterans Memorial is a monument in Washington, D.C., that honors Americans who served in the Korean War. It stands on the National Mall and includes 19 large statues of American combat troops in the Korean War, a circular Pool of Remembrance, and a commemorative mural wall.

The statues, sculpted by Frank C. Gaylord II, and made of stainless steel, stand from 7.25 to 7.5 feet (2.2 to 2.3 meters) tall. The combat troops are on patrol. They wear rain gear, symbolizing the Korean climate; and are trudging uphill on a bed of

The Korean War Veterans Memorial on the national mall in Washington, D.C., features 19 stainless steel statues of American combat troops in the Korean War. They wear rain gear, symbolizing the Korean climate; and are trudging uphill on a bed of evergreen shrubs, representing the rugged Korean terrain.

The memorial's commemorative mural wall, made of black granite, stands to the right of the statues. It extends 164 feet (50 meters) long. Pictures of about 2,500 U.S. military people who supported the combat troops in Korea are etched into the wall.

evergreen shrubs, representing the rugged Korean terrain. Their symbolic destination is an American flag on a flagpole in the distance.

The pool partially encircles the flag. It is surrounded by benches for visitors. The wall, designed by Louis Nelson and made of black granite, stands to the right of the statues. It extends 164 feet (50 meters) long. Pictures of about 2,500 U.S. military people who supported the combat troops in Korea are etched into the wall. The images include chaplains, clerks, doctors and nurses, engineers, and helicopter pilots. Dedicated in 1995, the monument is administered by the National Park Service.

Communists turn over UN troops at the prisoner of war (POW) receiving center at Panmunjon, on the border of North and South Korea. POW release to UN authorities was the first step in repatriation during the Korean War truce talks.

civilians. In 1953, the UN General Assembly expressed "grave concern" over these reports. However, the war ended without any war crimes trials.

After the armistice was signed, each side charged the other with torture and starvation of prisoners and other war crimes. The North Koreans and Chinese Communists were also accused of *brainwashing* prisoners. Brainwashing, or "thought reform," is forcibly changing a person's social, political, or religious beliefs through the systematic use of certain techniques. Chinese and North Korean forces used such methods in efforts to convert American prisoners to Communism. They isolated the prisoners, subjected them to severe physical hardship, and deprived them of sleep and other necessities. Such torment eventually caused a few prisoners to appear to give up their beliefs and accept those of their captors. The UN General Assembly adopted a general resolution condemning such acts. However, brainwashing has no formal

A convoy takes Chinese and North Korean POWs to Incheon, South Korea, on their journey to freedom during Operation Comeback. A military band welcomes them.

scientific basis. Many experts dispute that the practice is widespread or truly effective.

The UN Command and the Communists completed an exchange of 88,559 prisoners in September 1953. The Neutral Nations' Repatriation Commission took custody of prisoners who refused to return to their homelands. The armistice provided that delegates from the various countries could visit these prisoners and try to persuade them to go home. But 14,227 Chinese, 7,582 North Koreans, 325 South Koreans, 21 Americans, and 1 British prisoner refused to return. Some of these men later changed their minds.

After the war, the two sides remained hostile and suspicious of each other. In 1954, Soviet officials and representatives of countries that had fought in Korea met in Geneva, Switzerland. But the negotiators failed to draw up a permanent peace plan. Nor were they able to settle the question of unifying Korea.

## The Manchurian Candidate

*The Manchurian Candidate*, a motion picture released in 1962, is one of the most original political thrillers ever filmed in Hollywood. The movie describes how Raymond Shaw, an American soldier, is captured by the Communists during the Korean War and brainwashed to become an assassin on command. *The Manchurian Candidate* was directed by John Frankenheimer and starred Frank Sinatra in one of his most acclaimed dramatic performances. Sinatra played Bennett Marco, an American military investigator captured with Shaw in Korea.

*The Manchurian Candidate* mixes political satire, conspiracy and intrigue, humor, and suspense. The brainwashed soldier turns out to be the center of a plot to kill a presidential nominee. The plot is engineered by the soldier's mother, a vicious and ambitious woman. She wants to manipulate her husband, Shaw's stepfather and a United States senator, into becoming president of the United States.

Marco eventually uncovers the psychological plot involving Shaw and tries to convince him that his mind is being controlled by evil forces. At the last moment, instead of assassinating the presidential nominee, Shaw kills his mother and the senator and then takes his own life.

Audiences and critics praised *The Manchurian Candidate* for its engrossing storytelling and inventive editing and camera work, especially in portraying the nightmarish brainwashing scenes. In addition to Sinatra, the film starred Laurence Harvey as Shaw, Angela Lansbury as his mother, and James Gregory as the senator. Janet Leigh played Marco's sweetheart. Supporting players included John McGiver, Leslie Parrish, and Henry Silva. The film was adapt-

In *The Manchurian Candidate,* Laurence Harvey (standing right) starred as Raymond Shaw, an American soldier who is captured by the Communists during the Korean War and brainwashed to become an assassin on command.

ed from the best-selling 1959 novel by American writer Richard Condon.

A second motion picture version of *The Manchurian Candidate* was released in 2004, updating the setting from the Korean War to the Persian Gulf War of 1991. Denzel Washington played Marco, Liev Schreiber played Raymond Shaw, and Meryl Streep played Shaw's mother. Jonathan Demme was the director.

*North Korean soldiers march before a huge statue of former leader Kim Il-sung in Pyongyang. North Korea's military force is one of the largest in the world. Kim ruled North Korea from 1948, when the country was established, until his death in 1994.*

# CHAPTER FIVE

# A divided Korea

After the war, differences became stark between North and South Korea. The North Korean Communist leadership tightened its reins on the economy. Between 1953 and 1956, Kim Il-sung's government organized all farmland into collective farms. In 1954, it announced the first of a series of plans for economic development, all emphasizing heavy industry. North Korea also built up its military power. Kim's government operated as a strict dictatorship. Kim Il-sung remained in power until his death in 1994. North Korea has continued to maintain a dictatorship since then, first under Kim's son, Kim Jong-il (1942-2011) and then under his grandson, Kim Jong-un (1983?-    ).

South Korea had to rely heavily on aid from other countries after the war since fighting destroyed crops and factories and the country had little industry. The economic troubles of South Korea continued until the mid-1960's under the government of General Park Chung-hee (1917-1979).

South Korea's economy progressed rapidly under Park. His government concentrated on developing industries and increasing foreign trade. Park's economic programs called for the development of industries in various parts of the country, including Seoul. Until that time, Seoul had no major industry. Many new factories were built in Seoul during the 1960's and 1970's, and thousands of people moved there from rural areas to find work. Housing construction also boomed. New stores and restaurants opened, and various corporations built office buildings.

## Park Chung-hee

Park Chung-hee (1917-1979) served as president of South Korea from 1963 to 1979. He had taken power as head of the nation in 1961 after leading a military revolt against the civilian government. On Oct. 26, 1979, Park was assassinated by the head of the country's Central Intelligence Agency (now the National Intelligence Service).

Park, a controversial leader, helped establish many new industries in South Korea, and the country's economy grew rapidly under his rule. On the other hand, Park's government greatly restricted individual rights. For example, the government made it illegal to criticize the president or the constitution, which gave the president almost unlimited power. Park had many people imprisoned for criticizing his policies. He said harsh rule was needed to guard against attack by North Korea.

Park was born on Sept. 30, 1917, in Sonsan-gun, a county in North Gyeongbuk (also called Kyongsang) Province. In the early 1940's, he attended military academies and served in the Japanese Army. He entered the Korean Military Academy in 1945. Park became a Korean Army captain in 1946 and a general in 1953. After leading the 1961 military revolt, he headed a military government for two years. In 1963, Park resigned from the army and was elected president by the voters to head a new civilian government. He was reelected by the voters in 1967 and 1971. In

Major General Park Chung-hee (center) stands with his lieutenants in front of Seoul City Hall after seizing power in a coup on May 16, 1961. Park then became head of the new government.

1972 and 1978, Park was reelected by an electoral college made up of persons loyal to him.

In 2012, Park's daughter Park Geun-hye was elected to become South Korea's first woman president. She served from 2013 to 2017, when she was removed from office over accusations of corruption.

When the industrial and residential areas of Seoul became too crowded, construction of new factories and houses spread south of the Han River.

Busan's population increased sharply after the war, passing 3.4 million people. The city is an important center of South Korea's fishing industry. Busan has also become an administrative, commercial, industrial, and tourism center.

Incheon began to develop into a major industrial center in the late 1960's. Hundreds of factories went into operation in and around the city. Incheon's population soared after the industrial boom began.

Whereas Kim Il-sung ruled North Korea as a strict dictatorship, South Korea strove for a democratic government. Still, South Korea saw its early postwar leaders expand their executive powers and hold office for many years. Syngman Rhee remained as president for 12 years, until 1960, before resigning amid protests following his unopposed reelection. Park became head of government in 1961. He expanded his powers under a new constitution in 1972. He was assassinated in 1979.

In 1967, North Korean forces began making attacks in the Demilitarized Zone between the North and the South and into South Korea. In January 1968, North Korea seized the U.S. intelligence ship *Pueblo* in the East Sea (Sea of Japan). Also in 1968, about 30 North Korean troops raided Seoul in South Korea. They tried to assassinate South Korean President Park Chung-hee, but failed. In 1969, North Korea shot down a U.S. Navy plane almost 100 miles (160 kilometers) off the North Korean coast. In 1971, representatives of North and South Korea began formal reunification discussions for the first time since the Korean War.

After the war, thousands of U.S. troops were stationed in South Korea. In 1977—when about 38,000 troops remained—the United States government announced plans for a gradual withdrawal of all its troops. By mid-1979, about 10 percent of the troops had been withdrawn. But the United States government then said it would postpone further withdrawals until relations between North and South Korea improved. In 1981, U.S. President Ronald Reagan (1911-2004) announced that no more United States troops would be withdrawn.

In 1983, a bomb blast killed 17 South Koreans, including four cabinet ministers, during an official visit to Rangoon, Burma (now Yangon [*yahng GOHN*], Myanmar [*myahn MAHR*]). A court in Burma found North Korean agents guilty of the bombing. In 1988, South Korea hosted the Summer Olympics. North Korea refused to participate after its request to be named co-host was denied.

After the two governments agreed to accept each other's existence, an agreement to work toward the negotiation of a permanent peace treaty was signed by North and South Korea in 1991 and ratified in 1992. But in 1991, North Korea began to boycott the Military Armistice Commission, and China withdrew from the commission in 1994.

Also in 1991, talks resulted in several agreements, including a pact in which the two Koreas agreed not to use force against each other. As part of the pact, the two governments also agreed to increase trade and communication—which had been restricted—between them. Another accord prohibited North and South Korea from using or possessing nuclear weapons.

In 2000, Kim Jong-il met face-to-face in Pyongyang with South Korean President Kim Dae-jung (*kihm dy zhuhng*) to discuss relations. It was the first meeting between the leaders of North and South Korea since the peninsula was divided. As a result of this meeting, the two countries have made some additional moves toward improving relations. For example, some North Korean and South Korean relatives have been allowed to visit one another, and road and rail links have been reestab-

## Kim Jong-il

Kim Jong-il (*kihm zhong ihl*) (1942-2011) was the leader of North Korea from 1994 to 2011. He held the key posts of general secretary of the Workers' Party, North Korea's ruling Communist party; chairman of the National Defense Commission; and supreme commander of the People's Army. Kim Jong-il

succeeded his father, Kim Il-sung, who died in 1994. Kim Il-sung had, with Soviet support, established North Korea as a Communist state in 1948.

Kim Jong-il (also spelled Kim Chong-il) was born on Feb. 16, 1942, near Khabarovsk, in southeastern Russia (then part of the Soviet Union). He graduated from Kim Il-sung University in 1964. He then began moving up through the ranks of the Workers' Party. He gradually emerged as the leading interpreter of the party's principles and beliefs through his control of and support for North Korea's arts, especially filmmaking. In 1980, he was appointed to several top party offices. He used these posts and his father's support to strengthen his leadership in both the party and the army, paving the way for becoming his father's successor. In a similar manner, Kim Jong-il's youngest son, Kim Jong-un, was promoted to several top military and political offices in 2010.

The leaders of North and South Korea met in 2000 for the first time since Korea was divided. North Korea's leader, Kim Jong-il (left), greeted South Korea's president, Kim Dae-jung (right)

In 2000, Kim Jong-il held a summit with South Korea's leader, Kim Dae-jung. It was the first time the leaders of the two Koreas had met since the peninsula had been divided in 1948.

Kim Jong-il died on Dec. 17, 2011. The government preserved his body and placed it on display. Kim Jong-un succeeded his father as North Korea's leader.

lished between the two countries. In 2004, some South Korean companies began producing goods and employing North Korean workers in a special industrial zone in Kaesong, North Korea.

## Nuclear testing in North Korea

In 2002, North Korea held talks with Japan, the United States, and other countries in efforts to establish friendlier relations. However, these efforts were thrown into disarray when North Korea revealed that it had a secret program to develop nuclear weapons. The program violated North Korea's 1994 agreement with the United States. In late 2002 and early 2003, North Korea expelled international atomic energy inspectors from the country and reactivated its nuclear facilities. In 2006, the country tested a nuclear device, though experts believed the device was small. The test caused the United Nations to impose economic sanctions on North Korea.

In 2007, international talks resumed. North Korea agreed to shut down its main nuclear reactor and take steps toward dismantling its nuclear weapons program in return for fuel assistance. International atomic energy inspectors announced in July of that year that the reactor had been shut down, but the country failed to meet a December 31 deadline to provide full details of its nuclear program. In May 2008, the North Korean government turned over thousands of pages of documents relating to its nuclear program to U.S. inspectors. However, the U.S. government had not removed North Korea from its list of countries suspected of sponsoring terrorism, which had been a condition of the agreement. In September, North Korea began to restart the nuclear work it had halted. The United States removed the nation from its list in October, and North Korea again halted its nuclear work and allowed international inspectors to visit its reactor sites.

In a show of defiance on Independence Day in the United States,
North Korea launched a ballistic missile into the Sea of Japan on
July 4, 2017.

This photograph shows an elaborate festival in Pyongyang, North Korea's capital, celebrating the country's history and government.

In April 2009, North Korea tested a rocket that government officials claimed was intended to launch a satellite into orbit. However, some international affairs experts worried that it was actually a long-range missile test. The launch sparked international concern, and North Korea's government again expelled inspectors from its nuclear sites. North Korea refused to continue international talks on its nuclear program and announced that it had restarted its main nuclear reactor. In May, the country conducted further nuclear and missile tests.

Tensions between the Koreas increased in 2010. South Korea accused the North of sinking one of its warships with a torpedo in March while the ship patrolled the maritime border between the two countries. In November, North Korea fired artillery at an island claimed by South Korea.

North Korea again raised international concerns in December 2012, when it launched a rocket that put a satellite in orbit. Many international observers suspected that the event was a test of the country's ability to launch missiles capable of carrying nuclear warheads.

International concerns remained high after North Korea conducted another nuclear test in February 2013. Following the test, international tensions rose to their highest levels in years. South Korea withdrew its

A man in Seoul, South Korea, watches a television showing North Korean leader Kim Jong-un (center, in blue) celebrating a successful test launch of an intercontinental ballistic missile on July 29, 2017. Kim Jong-un said the test demonstrated the ability to strike targets in the United States—a direct retaliation for threats toward North Korea made by U.S. President Donald Trump.

## Kim Jong-un

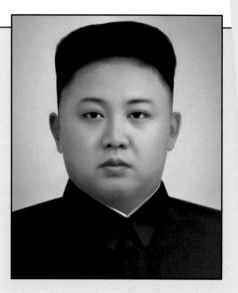

Kim Jong-un (1983?-    ) became the leader of North Korea in December 2011. He is the third leader of the country's *dynasty* (family of rulers). His grandfather Kim Il-sung established North Korea as a Communist state in 1948 and ruled until 1994. Kim Jong-un's father, Kim Jong-il, ruled from 1994 to 2011. Kim Jong-un came to power following his father's death on Dec. 17, 2011. He was named "supreme leader of the party, state, and army."

Little is known about Kim Jong-un's life. Many experts believe he was born on Jan. 8, 1983, though others believe he was born in 1982 or 1984. He is Kim Jong-il's third and youngest son. His mother was opera star Ko Young-hee, Kim Jong-il's third wife. Some experts believe Kim Jong-un attended school in Switzerland in the late 1990's and early 2000's. From 2002 to 2007, he studied military science at Kim Il-sung Military University in Pyongyang, North Korea's capital.

Experts believe Kim Jong-il prepared Kim Jong-un for leadership during the first decade of the 2000's. According to some intelligence reports, Kim Jong-un began working for the North Korean government in 2007. He is also believed to have become active in the country's ruling Communist party in that year.

North Korean leader Kim Jong-un (right) meets with Chung Eui-yong, director of the National Security Office for South Korean President Moon Jae-in, in March 2018. Kim holds a letter from Moon to arrange for more talks toward peace.

In 2010, Kim Jong-un was promoted to four-star general in the North Korean army. He also was named to the Communist party's Central Committee and became vice chairman of its Central Military Commission. These appointments led observers to believe that Kim Jong-il had chosen Kim Jong-un as North Korea's next leader.

workers from the Kaesong industrial complex for several months. The North Korean government issued threats against military bases in Japan, South Korea, and the United States. In April, the government announced that it would restart the nuclear reactor it had shut down in 2007.

In September 2015, North Korea's government announced that the country had restarted its nuclear program. North Korea continued testing nuclear devices and ballistic missiles in 2016 and 2017. As tensions increased, South Korea again pulled its workers from Kaesong.

## Recent developments in South Korea

In presidential elections in 2002, voters in South Korea elected Roh Moo-hyun, the candidate from Kim Dae-jung's Millennium Democratic Party (MDP). Roh took office in 2003. In September of that year, he left the MDP. In March 2004, South Korea's National Assembly voted to impeach Roh, accusing him of election law violations and incompetence. In elections in April, the Uri Party, which supported Roh, won a majority in the National Assembly. In May, South Korea's Constitutional Court overturned Roh's impeachment, and he was reinstated as president.

In late 2007, voters elected former Seoul Mayor Lee Myung-bak (*lee myuhng bahk*) to the presidency. He took office in February 2008. Corruption allegations against Roh continued, and Roh committed suicide in May 2009.

In December 2012, voters elected Park Geun-hye (*pahk goon heh*), daughter of former President Park Chung-hee, to become the country's first woman president. She took office in February 2013. In December 2016, South Korea's National Assembly voted to impeach her over allegations of corruption and abuse of power. In March 2017, the Constitution-

# Facts in brief about North Korea

**Capital:** Pyongyang.

**Official language:** Korean.

**Official name:** Choson-minjujuui-inmin-konghwaguk (Democratic People's Republic of Korea).

**Area:** 46,540 mi$^2$ (120,538 km$^2$), including islands and excluding the 487-mi$^2$ (1,262-km$^2$) Demilitarized Zone. *Greatest distances*—north-south, 370 mi (595 km); east-west, 320 mi (515 km). *Coastline*—665 mi (1,070 km).

**Elevation:** *Highest*—Paektu-san (Paektu Mountain), 9,003 ft (2,744 m) above sea level. *Lowest*—sea level.

**Population:** *Current estimate*—25,519,000; density, 548 per mi$^2$ (212 per km$^2$); distribution, 61 percent urban, 39 percent rural. 2008 census—24,052,231.

**Chief products:** *Agriculture*—apples, chickens, corn, potatoes, rice, soybeans. *Manufacturing*—chemicals, clothing, machinery, metals, military products, processed foods, textiles. *Mining*—coal, copper, iron ore, lead, magnesite, salt, tungsten, zinc. *Fishing*—pollock, shellfish, squid.

**Flag and coat of arms:** North Korea's flag has a horizontal red stripe between two thin white stripes on a blue background. The flag and coat of arms of North Korea have a red star that represents Communism. Rice and an electric power plant on the coat of arms stand for the importance of agriculture and industry to the North.

**Money:** *Basic unit*—North Korean won. One hundred chon equal one won.

**Form of government:** Communist.

**Climate:** Hot and wet in summer, cold and dry in winter.

## Kim Dae-jung

Kim Dae-jung (*kihm dy zhuhng*) (1924?-2009) served as president of South Korea from 1998 to 2003. Before he became president, Kim had run for the presidency several times but had always lost during a long career of opposition to South Korea's dictatorships. In 2000, Kim held a summit with North Korea's leader, Kim Jong-il. It was the first time the leaders of the two Koreas had met since the peninsula had been divided. Kim Dae-jung won the 2000 Nobel Peace Prize for his efforts to end hostility between North and South Korea.

Kim Dae-jung was born on Haui Island, off the southwest coast of South Korea. At different periods of his life, he had claimed to have been born on Jan. 6, 1924, or on Dec. 3, 1925. Some historians believe that the earlier date is likelier, and that he claimed the later date to avoid being drafted to fight for the Japanese during World War II. Kim studied economics at Kyung Hee University in Seoul. In the late 1940's, he started his own shipping company. In 1950, the Korean War began when troops from Communist-ruled North Korea invaded South Korea. Kim was arrested by the North Koreans as a "reactionary capitalist" and barely escaped execution by a firing squad.

After the war ended in 1953, Kim entered politics. Following several unsuccessful campaigns for a seat in the national legislature, he won election in 1960. In 1961, however, a group of military officers led by Park Chung-hee overthrew the South Korean government and dissolved the legislature. In 1963, Park restored the legislature. Kim was elected to a seat and won reelection in 1967. In 1971, Kim was defeated in a campaign against Park for the presidency. Many people charged that Park had won through fraud.

During the 1970's and early 1980's, Kim continued to speak out against a government that increasingly restricted the freedom of the South Korean people. He spent many months in prison and under house arrest. In 1982, he was forced to leave South Korea, and he moved to the United States. Kim returned to his country in 1985. He was defeated in presidential campaigns in 1987 and 1992, but was victorious in 1997. He took office in 1998. He stepped down in 2003. Kim died in Seoul on Aug. 18, 2009.

## Facts in brief about South Korea

**Capital:** Seoul.

**Official language:** Korean.

**Official name:** Taehan-min'guk (Republic of Korea).

**Area:** 38,713 mi$^2$ (100,266 km$^2$), including islands and excluding the 487-mi$^2$ (1,262-km$^2$) Demilitarized Zone. *Greatest distances*—north-south, 300 mi (480 km); east-west, 185 mi (298 km). *Coastline*—819 mi (1,318 km).

**Elevation:** *Highest*—Hallasan (Halla Mountain) 6,398 ft (1,950 m) above sea level. *Lowest*—sea level.

**Population:** *Current estimate*—50,869,000; density, 1,314 per mi$^2$ (507 per km$^2$); distribution, 83 percent urban, 17 percent rural. *2010 census*—51,069,375.

**Chief products:** *Agriculture*—barley, cabbages, chickens, dairy cattle, onions, rice, strawberries. *Manufacturing*—automobiles, chemicals, clothing, computer equipment, electric appliances, iron and steel, machinery, processed foods, rubber tires, ships, television sets, textiles. *Mining*—coal, iron ore. Fishing—anchovies, mackerel, squid, tuna.

**Flag and coat of arms:** South Korea's flag has a white background with a red-and-blue yin-yang symbol in the center. The ancient yin-yang symbol represents the balance in the universe between complementary forces—such as night and day, and life and death. There are four different I Ching symbols in each corner of the flag. In the coat of arms, yellow flowers encircle the yin-yang symbol.

**Money:** *Basic unit*—South Korean won.

**Form of government:** Republic.

**Climate:** Hot and wet in summer, cold and dry in winter. Seasonal winds called monsoons affect weather throughout the year. The east coast is less cold in winter.

The Opening Ceremony of the Olympic Games features the entry of the athletes into the stadium. Thousands of athletes, grouped by country, marched into the stadium at Pyeongchang, South Korea, on February 9 to officially begin the 2018 Winter Games. The athletes included the North Korea and South Korea Olympic teams, which entered together under a flag symbolizing a unified Korea.

al Court upheld the impeachment vote, and Park was removed from office. In May, voters elected former human rights lawyer Moon Jae-in (*moon jah ihn*) to the presidency.

In February 2018, North Korea participated in the Winter Olympic Games held in Pyeongchang, South Korea. North Korean and South Korean athletes marched together in the opening ceremony of the

## Park Geun-hye

Park Geun-hye (*pahk goon heh*) (1952-    ) was the first woman president of South Korea. She served from 2013 to 2017, when she was removed from office over accusations of corruption. Park led the conservative New Frontier (or Saenuri) Party, which was formerly the Grand National Party (GNP). She is the daughter of Park Chung-hee, who was president of South Korea from 1963 to 1979.

Park Geun-hye was born in Daegu (also spelled Taegu), South Korea, on Feb. 2, 1952. In 1961, Park Chung-hee led a successful military revolt against South Korea's civilian government. For two years, he headed a military government. In 1963, he resigned from the army and was elected president of a new civilian government. Under Park Chung-hee, South Korea's economy grew rapidly. However, he also greatly limited individual rights and kept a tight grip on power.

In 1970, Park Geun-hye graduated from Sacred Heart Girls' High School in Seoul. In 1974, she earned a bachelor's degree in electronic engineering from Sogang University in Seoul. She then moved to Paris to continue her studies. Her schooling was cut short, however, due to family tragedy. Her mother was killed on Aug. 15, 1974, in an attack that was intended to kill Park Chung-hee. Park Geun-hye returned to South Korea and became acting first lady. On Oct. 26, 1979, Park Chung-hee was assassinated by the head of the country's Central Intelligence Agency (now the National Intelligence Service).

After her father's assassination, Park Geun-hye stayed out of politics until she was elected to South Korea's National Assembly in 1998. From 2004 to 2006, she served as chairwoman of the GNP. In 2012, the GNP was renamed the New Frontier Party. That same year, Park Geun-hye was elected president. She took office in February 2013.

In 2016, hundreds of thousands of South Koreans protested against Park's rule after it was revealed that she had allowed a personal friend access to secret government documents. Park was also accused of helping to pressure South Korean companies to donate large sums of money to nonprofit foundations run by the friend. In December, South Korea's National Assembly voted to impeach Park over the scandal. In March 2017, the country's constitutional court upheld the parliamentary vote, and Park was removed from office. In May, voters elected former human rights lawyer Moon Jae-in to the presidency. In April 2018, Park was sentenced to 24 years in prison for abuse of power and corruption.

## Moon Jae-in

Moon Jae-in (*moon jah ihn*)
(1953-      ) is a lawyer and
politician who became president
of South Korea in May 2017. He
leads the liberal Democratic
Party of Korea. Moon succeeded
President Park Geun-hye, who
had been removed from office
after being accused of corruption.

Moon was born on the southern island of Geoje (also spelled
Koje), South Korea, on Jan. 24, 1953. His parents were refugees
who fled North Korea during the Korean War. His father then
worked at a camp for prisoners of war. His mother sold eggs.
Eventually, they settled in the port city of Busan (also spelled
Pusan).

In 1972, Moon began studying law at Kyung Hee University in
Seoul, the South Korean capital. He became a lawyer in 1980. In
1982, Moon and his friend Roh Moo-hyun opened a law firm in
Busan specializing in human rights cases.

Roh was elected president of South Korea in 2002 and served
from 2003 until 2008. Moon held several positions in the Roh
administration, including chief of staff. In 2012, Moon won a seat
representing Busan in the National Assembly. Later that year,
Moon ran for president but narrowly lost to Park Geun-hye.

In December 2016, the National Assembly voted to impeach
Park, and the Constitutional Court upheld the impeachment the

South Korean President Moon Jae-in (standing third from right) and U.S. Vice President Mike Pence (standing third from left) pose with officials and a Korean War veteran at the Korean War Veterans Memorial in Washington, D.C., in 2017.

following March. Fresh elections were held, and Moon won a decisive victory. His campaign focused on uniting the country in the wake of Park's corruption scandal. Moon also pledged to revive South Korea's economy and address the country's high youth unemployment rate.

Moon has expressed a willingness to negotiate with North Korean leader Kim Jong-un. Relations between the two Koreas remained poor after the Korean War and became increasingly tense in response to developments in the North's nuclear weapons program in the 1990's and early 2000's.

North Korea's leader Kim Jong-un (left) shakes hands with South Korea's President Moon Jae-in in April 2018 at the Military Demarcation Line in Panmunjom that separates their countries. The two leaders pledged to bring a formal end to the Korean War.

games and competed side by side on the Koreas' first joint Olympic team, in women's ice hockey. During the games, Kim Jong-un's sister Kim Yo-jong met several times with President Moon.

In April 2018, Moon and Kim Jong-un held a meeting at Panmunjom, in the Demilitarized Zone. At the meeting, the two leaders pledged to remove nuclear weapons from the Korean Peninsula and to work toward reaching a formal peace agreement to officially end the Korean War.

**FIND OUT MORE!**

Blohm, Craig E. *Cause and Effect: The Korean War.*
ReferencePoint, 2018.

Isserman, Maurice. *Korean War.* 3rd ed. Chelsea Hse., 2011.

Mitchell, Arthur H. *Understanding the Korean War: The
Participants, the Tactics, and the Course of
Conflict.* McFarland, 2013.

Tucker, Spencer C., and others, eds. *The Encyclopedia of
the Korean War: A Political, Social, and Military
History.* 3 vols. 2nd ed. ABC-CLIO, 2010.

## ACKNOWLEDGMENTS

| | |
|---|---|
| **Cover:** | U.S. Air Force; U.S. Marine Corps; © Bettmann/Getty Images |
| 4 | U.S. Navy |
| 6 | Two panels of an eight fold screen depicting *"A Story of Three Kingdoms"*, natural pigments on paper; Korean School/ Gahoe Museum/ Bridgeman Images |
| 9 | © Michele B, Shutterstock |
| 10 | WORLD BOOK map |
| 11 | Public Domain |
| 13 | © Giusparta/Shutterstock |
| 15 | © PhotoQuest/Getty Images |
| 16 | WORLD BOOK illustration |
| 19 | © Carl Mydans, The LIFE Picture Collection/Getty Images |
| 20 | Library of Congress |
| 22-23 | National Archives; Public Domain |
| 24 | National Archives |
| 26 | U.S. Marine Corps |
| 28 | U.S. Army |
| 30-31 | National Archives |
| 32 | Library of Congress |
| 34 | National Archives |
| 35 | WORLD BOOK map |
| 36 | © Carl Mydans, The LIFE Picture Collection/Getty Images |
| 38-39 | U.S. Navy |
| 41 | U.S. Army |
| 43 | National Archives |
| 44 | U.S. Marine Corps |
| 46 | WORLD BOOK map |
| 48-49 | U.S. Army; National Archives |
| 50 | WORLD BOOK map |
| 51 | WORLD BOOK map |
| 53 | © Topical Press Agency/ Getty Images |
| 55 | Department of Defense |
| 56-57 | U.S. Army; © San Francisco Chronicle |
| 58-61 | © Everett Historical/ Shutterstock |
| 62 | U.S. Marine Corps |
| 63-67 | U.S. Air Force |
| 69 | National Air and Space Museum |
| 71-77 | U.S. Navy |
| 78-79 | U.S. Air Force |
| 80 | © Bettmann/Getty Images |
| 82-83 | National Archives; Library of Congress |
| 84 | WORLD BOOK map |
| 86 | © Mattis Kaminer, Shutterstock |
| 88-89 | © Orhan Cam, Shutterstock; © Steve Heap, Shutterstock |
| 90-91 | U.S. Air Force |
| 93 | United Artists |
| 94 | © Dermot Tatlow, Panos Pictures |
| 96-101 | Public Domain |
| 103 | © STR/AFP/Getty Images |
| 104-105 | © Shutterstock; © Jung Yeon-Je, AFP/Getty Images |
| 106-107 | Public Domain; Blue House (Republic of Korea) |
| 109 | © Julia Sanders, Shutterstock; WORLD BOOK illustration |
| 110 | © Kim Jae-Hwan, AFP/ Getty Images |
| 112-113 | © Archivector/ Shutterstock; WORLD BOOK illustration; © Matthias Hangst, Getty Images |
| 114 | © Frederic Legrand, COMEO/Shutterstock |
| 116-117 | Jeon Han, Korean Culture and Information Service (licensed under CC BY 2.0); © Saul Loeb, AFP/ Getty Images |
| 118 | Republic of Korea |